What's HTML?

Learn It in 4 Hours

John Rouda

http://www.whatshtml.com

Editor: Abby Pritchard

First Edition

ISBN-13: 978-1480210363

ISBN-10: 1480210366

Table of Contents

Preface

Chapter 1 – What's HTML?

Chapter 2 – Getting the basics

Chapter 3 – In your HEAD

Chapter 4 – Text and Content

Chapter 5 – Anchor's Away

Chapter 6 – Picture Perfect

Chapter 7 – Lists and More Lists

Chapter 8 – It's all about Style

Chapter 9 – iFrames, Divs, and Tables

Chapter 10 – Simple Forms

Chapter 11 – HTML5

About the Author

Appendix A – HTML Reference

Appendix B – CSS Reference

Appendix C – HTML Entities

Preface

This book is designed to be a quick way to learn HTML and HTML5. It should also serve as a reference for you to look back on for refreshers and information on tags that are commonly used. This is a great resource for students and professionals that need a quick reference or wish to learn the basics of HTML quickly.

As a computer science professor, I've taught thousands of students HTML over the past ten years. I wrote this book to help teach others HTML in a simple easy to read format. For more HTML information, free instructor resources, and online tutorials visit http://www.whatshtml.com.

Chapter 1 – What's HTML?

Before you begin this book, it's important to understand what you should expect to get out of it. On any journey that we embark, we have to know the destination and the stops along the way. The intent of this book is to lay a foundation for learning about and developing websites using HTML. We'll cover the basics of HTML and web browsing and point you in the right direction to continue your learning experience.

We have also setup a website for you to go through additional tutorials and pose questions on our forum. You can find this additional information at http://www.whatshtml.com.

A Very Brief History of the Internet

The Internet was created in part as an experiment by the Defense Advanced Research Projects Agency (DARPA) for the U.S. Department of Defense (DoD). The first Internet was known as ARPANET, and computers were connected together of existing phone lines. By the end of 1969, four "host" computers were connected. By 1973, ARPANET had two international computers, one in London and one in Norway. In 1977, the first email application was generated, and then in 1984, the Domain Name System (DNS) was created. This innovation was significant because it allowed users to connect to a computer using a friendly name, like whatshtml.com, instead of an IP address. In 1990, the first web server was born.

Tim Berners-Lee, a British research scientist, invented a more efficient way of sharing information between computers, which is now known as "linking": He created the web. While at CERN, he created the standards for Hypertext Transfer Protocol (HTTP), Uniform Resource Identifier (URI), and Hypertext Markup Language (HTML). In this book, we'll be learning HTML.

Browser Basics

A web browser is a tool that is used to access information (web pages) located on the World Wide Web. There are several different popular web browsers that are available for free today. In order of popularity (at the time this book was written) the top five are: Chrome, Internet Explorer, Firefox, Safari, and Opera.

A browser reads and interprets the webpage code, downloads any needed associated files and displays the page in the best way it can interpret it. Most web browsers can read HTML, CSS, and JavaScript with no problems, however, some browsers may interpret some non-standard implementations of HTML in different ways.

For more information on browser basics, including some free tutorials, visit http://www.whatshtml.com.

Plugins

Most web browsers support the use of plugins. Plugins are mini-programs that are installed into your browsers to enable enhanced features. Chrome even has a web store to sell and offer free "app" style plugins. Adobe Flash is an example of a popular free plugin that can play certain types of media and animation. We will not be addressing any plugin development in this book, but it's good to know what a plugin is if you hear the term.

HTML Editors

HTML editors are just files that can be used to edit HTML documents. Any text editing software can be used to edit HTML files. HTML files are nothing more than plan text files that follow the HTML language structure and end in an .html or .htm file extension. On a Windows computer, Notepad would be a perfectly fine HTML editor for what we're doing in this book. On a Mac, TextEdit would suffice. For more advanced items and for some help with your coding, I would recommend a tool like Adobe DreamWeaver or Microsoft's Web Expression. These tools, along with many other what you see is what you get editors, can produce HTML on their own. Be careful when using these programs, as they are not guaranteed to produce 100% standard HTML every time. The use of these editors can lead to varying interpretations of the HTML in different browsers. It's always recommended to test everything out on different browsers before going public with it.

So What's HTML?

HTML is a markup language. An HTML file is really just a special type of text file. As we stated earlier, it can be edited in any standard text editor. By now, you probably remember that HTML stands for *Hyper Text Markup Language*, but what does that mean exactly? Let's break it down:

- **Hyper** is the opposite of linear. Old-fashioned computer programs were pretty much linear which means that they went in order, but with a "hyper" language, like HTML, the code can be run all at once, instead of going in linear order.
- **Text** is just made up of words written in plain English.
- **Markup** refers to the tags that are applied to the text to change its appearance. For instance, "marking up" your text with <b> before it and </b> after it make the text in bold.
- **Language** is a system of communication. HTML is a programming language that is interpreted by web browsers.

The Structure

The structure of an HTML document will be explained in more detail in the coming chapters. However, there are elements that every HTML document should contain: a <!DOCTYPE> which defines the type of document (remember, HTML is just a text document); a <html> section that wraps the entire page; a <head> section that contains formatting, scripting, and other information that isn't displayed on the screen; and a <body> section that contains the text and elements to be displayed on the screen. Example 1.1 shows the basic format of a webpage.

Example 1.1 – Basic format of a webpage

```
<!DOCTYPE html>
<html>
```

```
      <head>
            <title>My Webpage</title>
      </head>
      <body>
      <p>Stuff in the body of my webpage</p>
      </body>
</html>
```

Other Stuff

HTML documents usually contain other languages and items that aren't exactly HTML. Some of the other languages that are commonly included in HTML documents are Cascading Style Sheets (CSS) and JavaScript, a client-side scripting language. Over the past two decades, HTML has gone through several different versions and forms. Below is a chart showing the different versions and the year in which they came out.

Table 1.1

Version	Year	Version	Year
HTML	1991	HTML 4.01	1999
HTML+	1993	XHTML 1.0	2000
HTML 2.0	1995	HTML 5	2012
HTML 3.2	1997	XHTML 5	2013

HTML5

HTML5 is the newest version of HTML. It adds many new features and really streamlines large portions of the language. Since HTML really isn't going away, I'm going to address the new structure, added elements, and such in Chapter 11.

John Rouda

Chapter 2 – Getting the basics

In this chapter you'll learn the basic framework and structure of HTML. We'll also go over some simple rules and best practices. This chapter is vital for building the foundation and understanding the fundamentals of HTML. By the end of the chapter, you should be able to create a (very) simple webpage and view it in a browser.

HTML Tags

You've already learned the basic structure that every HTML page should follow (see Chapter 1), so now let's look at HTML tags. HTML tags are nothing more than keywords that are enclosed by *less than* and *greater than* signs, also known as angled brackets. HTML tags normally come in pairs: the start tag and the end tag. The start tag is the first one that opens a statement. The end tag is the second in the pair and closes the statement. The end tag also has a forward slash just after the *less than* sign letting you know that it is the end tag (see Example 2.1). The start tag, also called the opening tag, in this example is the <title> tag. After the content of the title (which shows up on your browser tab) is complete the tag is closed with an end tag, </title>.

Example 2.1 – Title Tag
<title>My First Webpage</title>

In this chapter, we're going to learn a few basic HTML tags. For a more complete list, see

Appendix A. An HTML tag can be broken down into three parts: an Element, an Attribute, and a Value.

HTML Elements

All HTML documents are defined by a collection of HTML *elements*. An HTML element is the start and end HTML tags and everything in between. Using Example 2.1 above, the HTML element would be "<title>My First Webpage</title>". Some HTML elements will not have any content between the start and end tags, while others will have loads of content, including other HTML elements. Many HTML elements will have *attributes* inside the opening (start) tag. Example 2.2 below has a paragraph tag which is setting the alignment to be centered by adding in an *align* attribute. This just centers the text between the two paragraph tags, similar to centering a paragraph of text in Microsoft Word. In this example, the *align*, is our attribute, and it is set to a value or *center*. You can change this paragraph setting by typing *align="center"* inside the opening paragraph tag.

Example 2.2 – Paragraph tag
<p align="center">This paragraph is aligned with the center of the page.</p>

Before we get too much further into HTML syntax, let's go over a few basic elements that are found in almost every webpage. In Chapter 1, we briefly mentioned the <html>, <head>, and <body> tags. Let's recap them real quick. The <html> element defines the entire document (webpage). The <body> element defines the body of the webpage that is viewable to the user. The <head> element defines a section where we'll add other elements which are not viewable (at least not directly) by the user. We'll cover this section in depth in the next chapter. Some other tags that are really important and found in almost every page that we should go over here are the <p> tag, the <a> tag, the <br> tag, the <hr> tag, and the <img> tag.

The <p> tag is your paragraph tag. This tag is used to define any paragraph of text that you're adding to a website. See Example 2.2 for its usage. The <a> tag is an anchor tag. The anchor tag is really important because it is used to define hyperlinks. A hyperlink is a word, phrase, or image that can jump you to another section, webpage, or website when you click on it. The <a> tag has a very important attribute that is defined as *href* and tells the page where to *link you* to when you click on it. See Example 2.3 below.

Example 2.3 – Anchor Tag
<a href="http://www.whatshtml.com">Click here to learn more about HTML</a>

The <br> tag is a line break tag. It adds in a blank line between text and images. This tag is a bit unique because it is a *self-closing* and empty tag. This means that there is no end tag needed. You can also write the <br> tag as <br/> which helps identify that it is a self-closing tag and doesn't need a closing tag present. Some HTML editors prefer it written the second way while others prefer it the first. Either way should work in any modern browser.

The <hr> tag is like the <br> tag. It is our *horizontal rule* tag. It is also an empty, self-closing tag and doesn't need an end tag. This tag adds a horizontal line across the page to break up text.

The <img> tag defines our image element. It is used to add images to a page. There are several attributes that can be used with the <img> tag which we'll cover in detail in Chapter 6. The basics of using the <img> tag can be seen below in Example 2.4.

Example 2.4 – Image tag
<img src="/images/pic1.jpg">

One thing you have to be sure you always remember to do is to close your tags. Many browsers are pretty forgiving on some tags, such as the paragraph tag, and they will operate as if closing the tag is optional. However, if you get into the habit of leaving tags open throughout your document, you'll end up leaving one that some browsers will not see as optional and the entire design of your page could be thrown off.

Whitespaces and Comments
In most cases, HTML will treat whitespace characters differently than other characters. HTML will *collapse* whitespace. This term means that a single whitespace character (spaces, tabs, and newlines) will be treated as a space, but a sequence of whitespace characters will be treated as a single whitespace character. I know that last sentence

was a bit confusing, so let me illustrate it below. The two paragraphs in Example 2.5 will display the text exactly the same (see Figure 2.1). The browser is *collapsing* the whitespace.

Example 2.5 - Spacing

<p align="center">This

paragraph
                is
        aligned with
        the
        center of the page.
</p>
<hr>
<p align="center">This paragraph is aligned with the center of the page. </p>

Figure 2.1

This paragraph is aligned with the center of the page.

This paragraph is aligned with the center of the page.

The next thing that we need to learn about is comments. If you're new to software development, comments are special elements added to code to describe the code and help anyone reviewing the code understand more about it. In HTML, comments are done by using the following syntax: <!—COMMENT GOES HERE -->.

The "COMMENT GOES HERE" portion can be anything that the developer wants it to be. Anything that is "Commented out," or between the <!—and --> tags will not display on the screen. See Example 2.6 for a sample of a comment.

Example 2.6 - Comments

<!-- This paragraph is centered at the request of Mr. Smith -->
<p align="center">This paragraph is aligned with the center of the page.</p>

Special Characters

HTML has something called special characters. Special characters are nothing more than characters that have been given special codes to represent them. They were given these codes because they are used as part of the HTML language themselves, so therefore it could be confusing if there were also allowed to be written as content on the page. Let me clear this up with an example. Let's say you were writing a webpage about HTML and you wanted to put your tags on the page to teach people about the <head> tag. Well, if you write something like <p>The <head> tag is used ...</p> you would get something like:

The tag is used...

Do you see the problem here? The browser can't determine that you are talking about the <head> tag, so it assumes that you are putting that tag in your code. Therefore, it doesn't display it to the end users. This confusion could have a very negative effect on the design and style of your site if you were writing about certain HTML elements. That's why special characters were created. These special characters are sometimes called HTML Entities. These HTML Entities can be called by using an entity name or an entity number. Entity names are designated by the ampersand (&) at the beginning and the semicolon (;) at the end, and entity numbers are designated by the &# at the beginning and the ; at the end. See Example 2.7.

Example 2.7 – HTML Entities

<p> The < head > tag is used... </p>

Example 2.7 would be displayed as:

The <head> tag is used....

For a complete list of HTML entities, see Appendix D.

Chapter 3 – It's In Your <head>

The head section of a webpage is usually placed just after the html tag. The head tag includes items that you don't want to show directly on the page but may be used to manipulate the page or browser window. The head section holds the title of the page, tags used for styling the content of the page, a storage location for script files, and a place to improve search engine optimization.

Title Tag

The <title> tag is a tag is used to display the title of a webpage in the top of the browser window above the standard tool bar (See Figure 3.1). The title tag is required for all HTML/XHTML web pages. The title tag is also used for the title of the page when it is saved to your favorites. Finally, the title tag is used to display the title of the page on search engines and is essential for proper search engine optimization. The proper syntax for the title tag would be as follows:

Example 3.1 – The Title Tag
<title>My First Webpage</title>

Figure 3.1 – The Title Tag

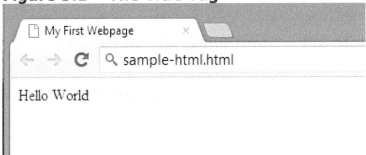

Meta tags

The head section also includes elements that can help describe the page and the contents on the page to search engines. These are called meta tags (<meta>). Meta tags can be used for many different things other than just search engine optimization. Meta tags always go inside of the head section and are always used with attributes and values. Most meta tags use either the *name* attribute or the *http-equiv* attribute. There is also a *content* attribute that is used in conjunction with the *name* or *http-equiv* attributes, but the *content* attribute cannot be used without the name or *http-equiv* attribute. Below are some examples of meta tags that use the *name* and *content* attributes:

Example 3.2 – Identifying keywords for a webpage

<meta name ="keywords" content="HTML, Learning, CSS, Book">

Example 3.3 – Identifying a description for a webpage

```
<meta name="description" content="Learn HTML and
CSS">
```

Example 3.4 – Identifying the webpage's author

```
<meta name="author" content="John Rouda">
```

The *http-equiv* attribute has three different values that can be used in conjunction with it. These are *content-type, default-style,* and *refresh.* The *content-type* attribute is used to define the character encoding used for the webpage.

Example 3.5 – Character encoding

```
<meta http-equiv="content-type"
content="text/html;charset=UTF-8">
```

The *default-style* attribute isn't used very often but can be used to specify a preferred style sheet to use on the webpage. Many web page developers choose to link the style sheet to the page using a different method that we'll cover later in this chapter.

Example 3.6 – Preferred style sheet

```
<meta http-equiv="default-style"
content="/css/style.css">
```

The meta *refresh* element is used to either automatically refresh a webpage after a given time interval or to redirect the webpage to a different

location. Below are two examples of the meta
refresh element:

Example 3.7 – Refresh the page every 30 seconds

<meta http-equiv="refresh" content="30">

Example 3.8 – Redirect the page after 1 second

*<meta http-equiv="refresh"
content="1;url="http://www.johnrouda.com/">*

Table 3.1 – Meta attributes and values

Attribute	Values	Description
name	author description keywords generator application-name	Identifies the name of the meta date defined in the tag.
content	*any text*	Specifies a value associated to the *name* or *http-equiv* attributes in the tag.
http-equiv	content-type default-style refresh	Creates an HTTP header for the value of the associated

		content attribute in the tag.
charset (*new to HTML5*)	*any character set*	Identifies the character encoding used for the webpage.

Link Tag

The link tag does pretty much what you would expect it to do: it links a document with an external source. The <link> tag used mostly to link to external style sheets. Below is an example of this type of use:

Example 3.9 – Linking a style sheet

```
<link rel="stylesheet" type="text/css"
href="/css/styles.css">
```

The link tag, like the meta tag, has several attributes and values that allow it to do different things when linking to an object. For a brief overview of these, please see Table 3.2.

Table 3.2 – Link attributes and values

Attribute	Values	Description
href	*any URL*	Identifies the location of the linked document.
hreflang	*any language*	Identifies the

	code	language of the linked document.
media	all, aural, braille, handheld, projection, print, screen, tty, tv	Identifies on what device the linked document will be applied (displayed).
sizes (*new to html5*)	*height x width* or *any*	Identifies the size of the linked item. Only used for rel="icon".
target (**not supported in html5**)	_blank _self _top _parent *frame name*	Identifies the target of the linked document.
type	application, audio, example, image, message, model, multipart, text, video	Identifies the MIME media type of the linked resource.

Base Tag

The base tag is used to define the base folder path or location for the relative location of linked items on a webpage. Using the target attribute, the base tag can also define the default target for all links. For example, using a target of *_blank* will cause linked documents to open in a new window, including hyperlinks, images, and style sheets. The base tag should be used as your first element in your <head> section, so that all other elements can follow the set relative path defined by the base. A base tag must include either a *href* attribute or a *target* attribute or both. Below is an example of how it can be used:

Example 3.10 – The base tag

```
<base href="http://www.johnrouda.com/images/"
target="_blank">
```

Script Tag

The script tag is a tag that is used to define a client-side script, such as JavaScript. Client-side scripts are just scripts that run in the end-users' browser and not on the web server that hosts the HTML webpage. The script tag can either contain the actual scripting statements, or it can link to an external script file using the *src* attribute. JavaScript is the most common client-side scripting language and is commonly used for image manipulation, dynamic changes to content, loading media, changing styles, and form validation. If the *src* attribute is set, then the script element must be empty and cannot contain any type of scripting statements. Below are two examples of the use of the script tag:

Example 3.11 – The script tag for an external source

```
<script type="text/javascript"
src="myscripts.js"></script>
```

Example 3.12 – The script tag with scripting statements

```
<script>
      document.write("Hello World!")
</script>
```

The script tag has several attributes that you can read more about in Table 3.3. One attribute in this table that is new to HTML5. It is the *async* attribute. The *async* attribute is used to determine how external scripts are executed. There are three ways that an external script can be executed. If *async="async"* then the script will be executed asynchronously with the rest of the page, i.e while the page continues to be parsed. If *defer="defer"* then the script will be executed when the page finishes its parsing. If *async* is not set or set to anything else, then the script is executed immediately before the rest of the page is parsed.

There is also a *noscript* tag that can be used for users that have disabled client-side scripting or that have browsers that do not support script tags.

Table 3.3 – Script attributes and values

Attribute	Values	Description
Type	text/javascript *(this is default)* text/ecmascript application/ecmascript application/javascript text/vbscript	Identifies the MIME type of the external script file.
Src	*any URL*	Identifies the location of the linked document.
Defer	defer	Identifies what device the linked document will be applied (displayed).
async (*new to html5*)	async	Identifies the size of the linked item. Only used for rel="icon".
Charset	*Any character set*	Indentifies the character encoding for the external script file.

Style Tag

The style tag allows you to define style information in a particular webpage. I would not recommend using this for most websites. Using linked style sheets as described in the link tag section is the preferred method. Linking to an external style sheet lets you reuse the style sheet on a number of pages. It also allows for browser caching and easy updates. Below is an example of simple style tag that is used to set the background color, font, and font color.

Example 3.13 – The style tag

```
<style type="text/css">

        body {background-color:#b0c4de;
        font-family:arial, verdana;
        color:#00ff00;}

</style>
```

Chapter 4 – Text and Content

What good is a website without content? Text and content show us all we need to know about content. The HTML code instructs the browser how a webpage should appear, and a good appearance helps draw the attention of the reader. Proper formatting is the key to make your webpage fresh, clean, and attractive. Let's learn some formatting tags for your text in HTML.

Heading tag

A web page should start with heading tags. There are different types of sizes available for headings ranging from <h1> to <h6>. The heading element <h1> indicates the weighty headings and <h6> indicates the minor headings. Headings are also used for webpage indexing by various search engines. Each heading must start with an opening heading tag <h> and ends with a closing heading tag</h>

Example 4.1 – Heading Tag

```
<!DOCTYPE html>
<html>
<body>
<h1>Weighty Heading</h1>
<h2>Heading 2</h2>
<h3>Heading 3</h3>
<h4>Heading 4</h4>
<h5>Heading 5</h5>
<h6>Minor Heading</h6>
```

```
</body>
</html>
```

Figure 4.1. – Heading Tag

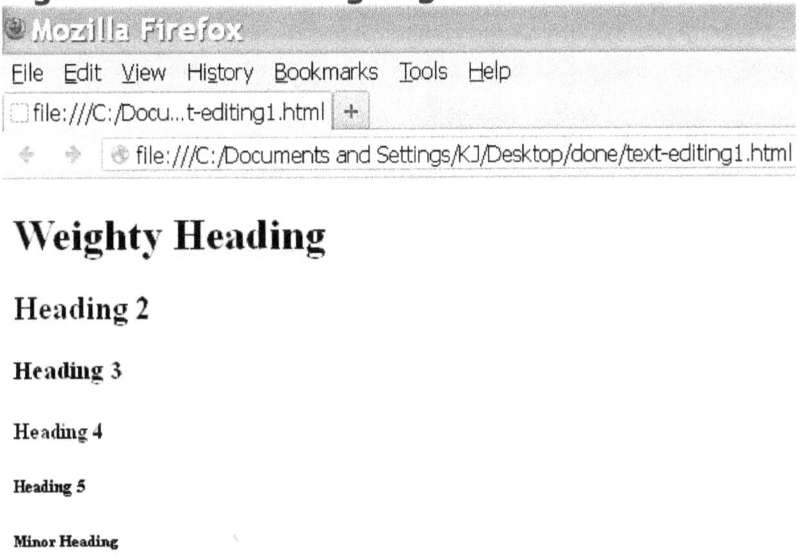

Paragraphs

HTML provides paragraph tags <p> which adjust the line spacing between the lines in paragraph and line spacing among the paragraphs. The default spacing between lines in paragraph is single space and between the paragraphs is double space. Paragraph must begin with an opening paragraph tag <p> and ends with closing paragraph tag </p>.

Example 4.2 - Paragraphs

```
<!DOCTYPE html>
<html>
<body>
<p>HTML provides Paragraph tags which
adjusts the line spacing between the lines in
paragraph and line spacing among the
paragraphs.</p>
<p>The default spacing between lines in
paragraph is single space and between the
paragraphs is double space.</p>
</body>
</html>
```

Figure 4.2. Paragraphs

HTML provides Paragraph tags which adjusts the line spacing between the lines in paragraph and line spacing among the paragraphs.

The default spacing between lines in paragraph is single space and between the paragraphs is double space.

Paragraphs can also be aligned using the align attribute. The values of align attribute can be left, right, center, and justify.

Example 4.3 - Alignment

```
<!DOCTYPE html>
<html>
<body>
```

```
        <p align="left"> This is an example of
paragraph with left alignment</p>
        <p align="right"> This is an example of
paragraph with right alignment</p>
        <p align="center"> This is an example of
paragraph with center alignment
        </p>
        <p align="justify">
        This is an example of paragraph with justify
alignment </p>.

        </body>
        </html>
```

Figure 4.3 - Alignment

Blockquote

In HTML, Blockquote is used for distinguishing a few lines or paragraph which are extracted from another source, either quoted by a person or document. According to W3C webpage, you must not use quotation marks when using Blockquote, but in practice, webpage authors still include quotation marks. Blockquote must begin with an opening blockquote tag <blockquote> and end with closing blockquote tag </ blockquote >.

Most browsers indent the Blockquote paragraph with left or right alignment. As a result, many authors use Blockquote to indent their text to attract the reader to the paragraph.

In reality, Blockquote should only be used if a paragraph is extracted from other source.

Example 4.3 - Blockquote

```
<!DOCTYPE html>
<html>
<body>

<h1> Marquee Tag </h1>

<p>Here is a quote from codingmanual
website:</p>

<blockquote cite="http://www.
http://www.codingmanuals.com/html-
tutorials/marquee/ ">
        Marquee: This tag is used to
display text in a scrolling way on a
webpage. You must have seen many
sites using this moving text; it does
grab some attention from the user.
The attributes of this tag are Direction,
Behavior, and Loop.
1) Direction: It specifies whether the
text scrolls from right to left or left to
right.
```

What's HTML? Learn It in 4 hours

2) Behavior: Behavior has three values: scroll, alternate, and slide. Scroll causes moving of text from left to right or vice versa. Alternate causes text to bounce back and forth between the margins. Marquee slides through the webpage because of slide value. The default value is scroll.
3) Loop: It tells the number of times marquee should scroll.
</blockquote>

</body>
</html>

Figure 4.3 - Blockquote

Preformatted Text

Preformatted text tag (<pre>) allows webpage text to appear in the same format as it is written in HTML document. Preformatted text tag (<pre>) must begin with an opening tag <pre> and ends with closing pre tag </ pre >. The browser restores text inside the opening and closing preformatted text tag in the same format in terms of character and line spacing as written in HTML document. All the text inside the <pre> and </pre> tags are displayed in monospaced font by the browser. The preformatted text tag should be used to preserve the integrity of columns and rows of characters.

Example 4.4 – Pre Tag

```
<!DOCTYPE html>
<html>
<body>

<pre>
#include <stdio.h>

int main()
{
        printf("Hello world\n");
        return 0;
}
</pre>

</body>
</html>
```

Figure 4.4 – Pre Tag

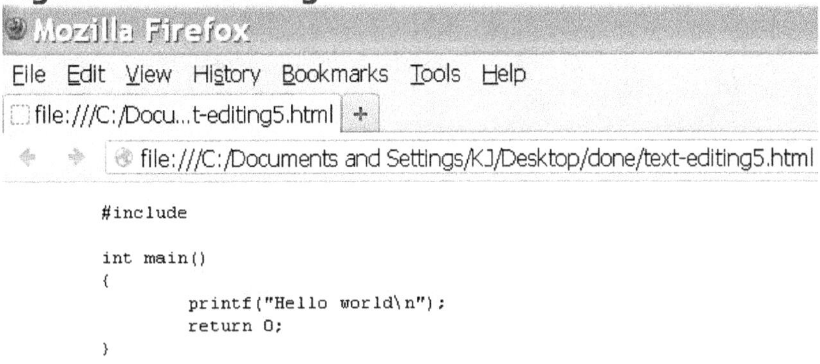

Mozilla Firefox

File   Edit   View   History   Bookmarks   Tools   Help

file:///C:/Docu...t-editing5.html   +

file:///C:/Documents and Settings/KJ/Desktop/done/text-editing5.html

```
#include

int main()
{
        printf("Hello world\n");
        return 0;
}
```

Line Breaks

As the name indicates, a line break tag <br> is used to end any line. Anything which is written after a <br> tag appears on the next line. There are no opening and closing tags in a line break.

Example 4.5 – Line breaks

```
<!DOCTYPE html>
<html>
<body>

<p>
This is <br>an example,<br>of a line break tag.
</p>

</body>
</html>
```

John Rouda

Figure 4.5 – Line breaks

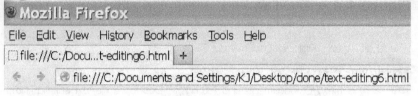

This is
an example,
of linebreak tag.

Horizontal Rule

The Horizontal rule <hr> tag is used to display a horizontal rule in a webpage. The Horizontal rule <hr> tag doesn't have any end tag. It basically used to separate the content of a HTML code.

Example 4.6 – HR tag

```
!DOCTYPE html>
<html>
<body>

<h1>HTML</h1>
<p>HTML is a Hyper Text Markup Language
.</p>

<hr>

<h1>CSS</h1>
<p>CSS is Cascading Style Sheets.</p>

</body>
```

```
</html>
```

Figure 4.6 –HR tag

HTML

HTML is a Hyper Text Markup Language .

CSS

CSS is Cascading Style Sheets.

Ordered List

As name indicates, the Ordered list <ol> tag displays an ordered list. And each list item should start with list item tag <li>. An ordered list can be numerical or alphabetical.

Example 4.7 – OL example
```
<!DOCTYPE html>
<html>
<body>
<h3>Shopping List </h3>
<p> Fruits </p>
<ol>
  <li>Orange</li>
  <li>Mango</li>
```

```html
   <li>Banana</li>
</ol>
<p> Vegetables </p>
<ol type="I" >
 <li>Brinjal</li>
 <li>Tomato</li>
 <li>potato</li>
</ol>

<h3> Phone Book </h3>
<ol type="A" >
<li>32356562</li>
<li>99888765</li>
<li>87967845</li>
</ol>
</body>
</html>
```

Figure 4.7 – OL example

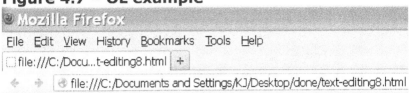

Shopping List

Fruits

1. Orange
2. Mango
3. Banana

Vegetables

I. Brinjal
II. Tomato
III. potato

Phone Book

A. 32356562
B. 99888765
C. 87967845

Unordered lists

Unordered lists tags (<ul>) are same as ordered lists tags (<ol>), and the only difference is that they use bullets instead of numbers or alphabets before list item<li>. Unordered lists tag (<ul>)   is used in non-sequential items. The default bullet type is disc, but the user can define others too.

Example 4.8 – UL example

```
<!DOCTYPE html>
<html>
<body>

<h4>An Unordered List:</h4>
<ul>
  <li>Fruits</li>
  <li>Vegetables</li>
  <li>Milk</li>
</ul>

</body>
</html>
```

Figure 4.8 – UL example

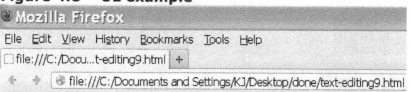

An Unordered List:

- Fruits
- Vegetables
- Milk

The <strong> tag

An important text is displayed by using <strong> tag.

The <em> tag

To display an emphasis on text, we use <em> tag.

Bold tag <b>

To display the text in bold, we use bold tag <b>. Any text between opening bold tag <b> and closing bold tag </b> is displayed as bold.

Italic tag <i>

To display the text in Italic, we use Italic tag <i>. Any text between opening Italic tag <i> and closing Italic tag </i> is displayed as Italic.

Underline tag <u>

To display the text with an underline, we use underline tag<u>. Any text between an opening underline tag <u> and closing underline tag </u> is displayed as underlined.

Subscript tag <sub>

The <sub> tag is used to display the subscripted text. Subscript text is half a character below the baseline and can be used for writing the chemical formulas.

Superscript tag <sup>

The <sup> tag is used to display the superscripted text. Superscript text is half a character above the baseline and can be used for writing the mathematical formulas.

Strike tag <strike>

To display the text with a strikethrough we use strike tag<strike>. Any text between opening strike tag <strike>and closing strike tag <strike> is displayed as text with a thin line passing through center of text.

<big> tag

The <big> tag is used to display text with a bigger size as compared the other text.

<small> tag

The <small> tag is used to display text with a smaller size compared the other text.

<code> tag

The <code> tag displays the text as a piece of computer code.

Example 4.9 – Tag examples

```
<!DOCTYPE html>
<html>
```

```
<body>
<p>An example of <strong>Strong
Text</strong></p>
<p>An example of <em>Emphasized
Text</em></p>
<p>An example of <b>Bold Text</b></p>
<p>An example of <i>Italic Text</i></p>
<p>An example of <u>Underline
Text</u></p>
<p>An example of <sub>subscripted
Text</sub></p>
<p>An example of <sup>superscripted
Text</sup></p>
<p>An example of <strike>strikethrough
Text</strike></p>
<p>This text is normal.<big>This text is
bigger.</big></p>
<p>This text is normal.<small>This text is
smaller.</small></p>
<p>An example of <code>Computer Code
Text</code></p>
</body>
</html>
```

Figure 4.9 – Tag examples

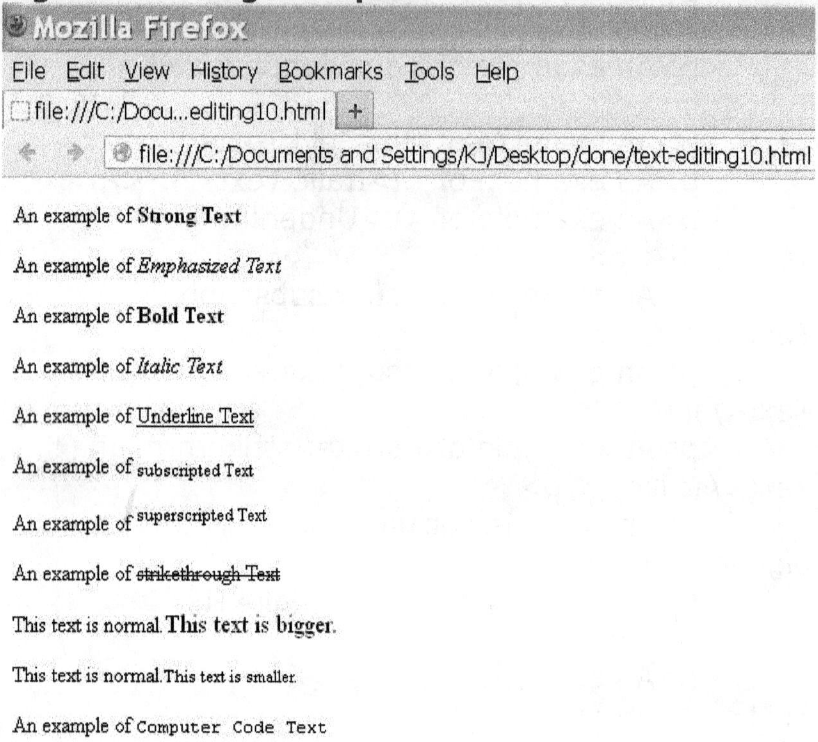
Mozilla Firefox
File Edit View History Bookmarks Tools Help
file:///C:/Docu...editing10.html
file:///C:/Documents and Settings/KJ/Desktop/done/text-editing10.html
An example of Strong Text
An example of Emphasized Text
An example of Bold Text
An example of Italic Text
An example of Underline Text
An example of subscripted Text
An example of superscripted Text
An example of strikethrough Text
This text is normal. This text is bigger.
This text is normal. This text is smaller.
An example of Computer Code Text

Chapter 5 – Anchor's Away

An anchor or hyperlink, commonly known as *link*, is either a word or group of words in webpage which are connected to another webpage. Hyperlinks can be connected to anything such as other Web pages, file downloads, viewing a movie, listening to music, or emails. Let's learn some more about hyperlinks.

How to hyperlink a webpage?

An Anchor tag<a> is used to create a hyperlink. Basically, an anchor tag needs only one attribute known as Hypertext REFerence attribute of the anchor tag (href) and the hypertext (text which will contain the hyperlink) . Anchor tags should end with a closing anchor tag </a>.

Example 5.1 – hyperlink example

```
<!DOCTYPE html>
<html>
<body>

 For more details log on <a
href="http://www.example.com">
www.example.com </a>

</body>
</html>
```

Figure 5.1 –hyperlink example

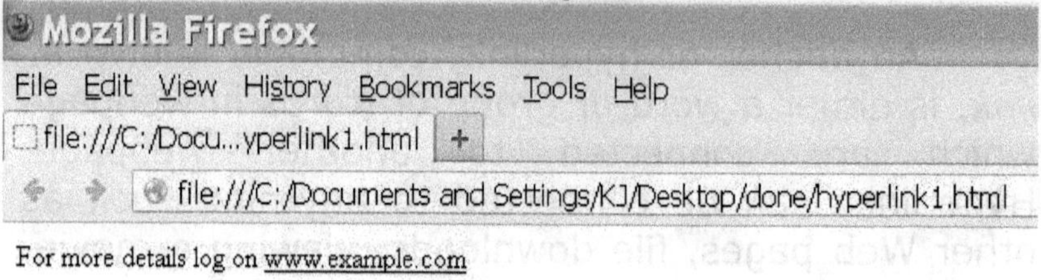

For more details log on www.example.com

In the above example, the value of href is the URL of the destination webpage and here is hypertext.

There are few additional attributes for anchor tags which specify whether the new document should open in new browser window, relationship among the Web pages, etc.

Usually, hyperlink opens the destination page within the same browser window. In other words, the main webpage is replaced by the destination webpage. If we want the hyperlink to open in a new window and the main webpage should remain in the browser window, we should add target="_blank" in the anchor tag <a>.

Example 5.2 – Target Attribute

To open the tutorial.html file in a new window of the browser:

```
<!DOCTYPE html>
<html>
```

```
<body>


Complete <a href=" tutorial.htm"
target="_blank">HTML tutorials </a> that
covers from basics up to css.
</body>
</html>
```

Figure 5.2 – Target Attribute

Complete HTML tutorials that covers from basics up to css.

Let's learn something about the URL paths provided to Hypertext Reference attribute of the anchor tag.

The URL paths that are provided can be either absolute path or relative path. Absolute path has the complete address of the targeted destination page. Absolute paths are trustworthy the only drawback is that they are very long and so difficult to remember.

Example 5.3 – URL path

```
<!DOCTYPE html>
```

```
<html>
<body>

<a
href="http://example/subjects/tutorial.html">
HTML tutorials</a>

</body>
</html>
```

Figure 5.3 – URL path

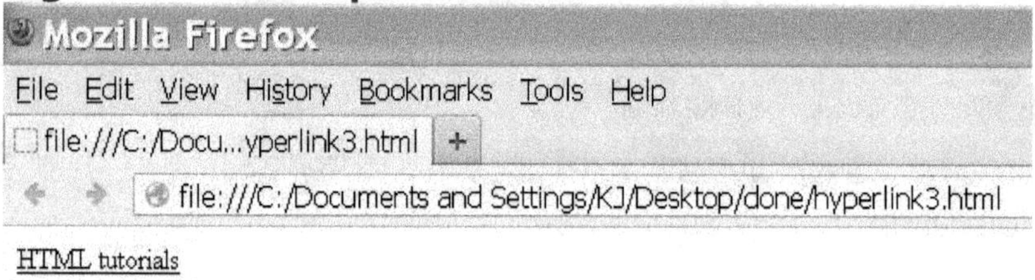

In the case of linking two files of same website, we do not need to specify the complete path of the file rather we can directly state its name. This is called a relative path, as the destination file is relative to the current file location. Relative paths are shorter and easy to remember.

Can we choose the link colors?

Hyperlinks should be distinct from the other words of the document. They should be recognized by users. There are four different link status modes. They are link, active, visited, and hover.

1) **Link**: The hyperlink that points to the desired document which is neither opened in browser nor visited before.
2) **Active**: The hyperlink is clicked and is open in the browser.
3) **Visited**: The desired document has been viewed previously or can be found in the browser's cache.
4) **Hover**: The mouse pointer is on the hyperlink text.

Each of the above mentioned link status modes should be different is color so that the user can identify the status of the modes of each and every link on the Webpage.

- Hyperlink in link mode is blue in color and its hypertext is underlined.
- Hyperlink in Active mode is red in color and its hypertext is underlined.
- Hyperlink in visited mode is purple in color and its hypertext is underlined.
- Hyperlink in hover mode does not show any change.

If we want to change the hypertext color and other attributes of the hyperlink, we can do it by changing the default properties of each type of anchor tag.

Example 5.4 – Hyperlink Colors

```
<!DOCTYPE html>
<html>
<body>

<a href="http://www.example.com">Visit
example.com!</a>

<STYLE TYPE="text/css">
a:link { color: green; text-decoration:
underline}
a:visited { color: red; text-decoration:
underline}
</STYLE>

</body>
</html>
```

Figure 5.4 - Hyperlink Colors

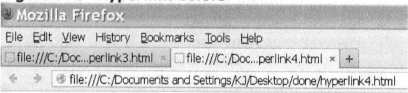

In the above example, the color of text displayed in the hypertext of visited hyperlink will be red in color.

Hyperlinking To an E-Mail Address

Hyperlinking to an email is used when multiple webpage users are directed to send an email to the same person. To make a hyperlink to email you should add mailto attribute in href.

Example 5.5 –Email links

```
<!DOCTYPE html>
<html>
<body>

<a href=mailto:support@example.com >
Contact Us </a>

</body>
</html>
```

Figure 5.5 – email links

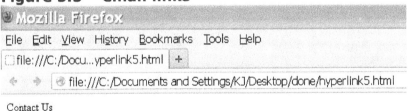

Hyperlinking to an email is supported by most browsers, so it is advisable to display the address as hypertext.

Example 5.6 – Email link 2

```
<!DOCTYPE html>
<html>
<body>

Contact Us at <a
href="mailto:support@example.com">support@exa
mple.com</a>

</body>
</html>
```

Figure 5.6 –Email link 2

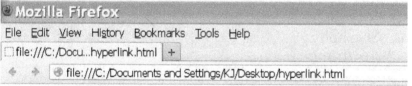

The main disadvantage of hyperlinking an email address is receiving large number of junk emails, so it is advisable to put your alternate email address on the public webpage.

Create an Anchor

Anchors can also be used as marker in the webpage that directly links to the desired target. For a deeper understanding, let's imagine that there is a large document with various sections. Suppose we need to read about a section which is discussed at the bottom, so we need to scroll through the whole page and read the desired section. Now, instead of doing this, we can create links to each section and place it on the top so that we can easily read the desired section without going through the whole page. This can be done using an anchor.

To create an anchor, we need to use the name attribute in anchor tag. There are some other attributes of anchor: charset, type, name, href, hreflang, rel, rev, accesskey, shape, cords, tabindex, onfocus, and onblur. The charset attribute defines encoding while type expresses the type of element. Name describes anchor name, and href defines desired URL. Rel describes forward link type (hyperlink relationship) while rev outlines reverse link type (hyperlink relationship). Shape defines the shape of clickable area, i.e. rectangle, circle, or polygon. Cords express the coordinates of the shape of clickable area (If the clickable area is a rectangle, then four coordinates; if it's a circle, then the coordinate of center of circle and coordinates of the radius).

Example 5.7.1 – Anchor Tag

```
<a name="Marquee tag"> Marquee tag</a>
```

In the above code, we have created an anchor as Marquee tag. Now we need to link this anchor to the desired destination, so assign the href attribute with the desired url and add a hash sign along with the anchor name at the end of url.

Example 5.7.2 – Anchor Tag

```
<!DOCTYPE html>
<html>
<body>
<a href="http://www. Example.com #Marquee
tag"> Marquee tag</a>
</body>
</html>
```

Figure 5.7 – Anchor Tag

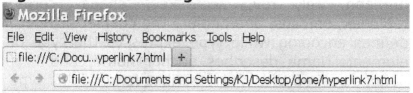

In the above example, Marquee tag will appear as anchor at the webpage and is linked to the desired destination.

Is it possible to hyperlink to other content on internet?

A hyperlink can access any file on the Web. We can create a link to Microsoft Office documents, executable program (.exe files), zip files, and any other utility programs that are needed by the visitors.

Linking to other content is same as linking to a Web page. We should think about few things before creating a link to non-HTML content.

Linking must be user friendly; we must not link to utility which is sparsely used, not all users are using the same software.

Example:
Suppose we are providing a link to an executable file but before that we must also think about its requirements. How many users can fulfill the requirements? What about the remaining users? There are browsers which automatically try to download the suitable application (plug-in, viewer, etc.) for displaying the file or executing the file, but there may be users who are using a different browser which does not provide such facility.

In such cases, we should provide a hyperlink to a free application which can run that file.

Chapter 6 – Picture Perfect

I'm going to spend a little bit of this chapter talking about graphics, UI/UX (User Interface / User Experience), and best practices. The actual HTML part of adding images and background images is pretty straight forward.

Typically, we use one of the following three types of image formats: Graphic Interchange Format (GIF), Joint Photographic Expert Group (JPEG), and Portable Network Graphic (PNG).

In HTML, images can be added into the webpage using <img> tag. The <img> tag needs at least two attributes: the first attribute is alt and the other is source (src). The <img> tag does not require a closing tag.

The alt attribute defines the alternate text that will be displayed if the image cannot be displayed. It provides more information about the image if the image cannot be loaded for some reason (poor inter connectivity or error in src attribute).

Source (src) is the location at which the required image is stored, so the value of src is the image URL that we want to display.

To add an image to your HTML webpage, you use the following code.

Example 6.1 – Image Tag

```
<!DOCTYPE html>
<html>
<body>


<img alt="Rare Flower"
src="http://www.example.com/flower.jpg"> [
Source Link has to be the actual file path of the
picture]

</body>
</html>
```

Image Alignment

Mostly the image is displayed before or after the text according to the location where <img> tag is written in the code. The browser wraps the image onto the next line if the image does not fit in the current line according to the formatting and paragraph's alignment. The image can be aligned with reference to the other objects nearby. The image can be align using the align attribute in the <img> tag. The align attribute can have the following values.

1) **Top**: Image can be aligned at the top of nearby text or object.
2) **Bottom**: Image can be aligned at the bottom of nearby text or object.
3) **Middle**: Image can be aligned at the middle of nearby text or object.

4) **Left**: Image can be aligned to the left of nearby text or object.
5) **Right**: Image can be aligned to the right of nearby text or object.

The default alignment of an image is bottom.

Example 6.2 – Image Example 2

```
<!DOCTYPE html>
<html>
<body>

<h4> Image with default alignment
(align="bottom"):</h4>
<p> Do not worry <img src="smiley.gif"
alt="Smiley face" width="32" height="32"> Be
happy</p>

<h4> Image with align="middle":</h4>
<p> Do not worry <img src="smiley.gif"
alt="Smiley face" align="middle" width="32"
height="32"> Be Happy</p>

<h4> Image with align="top":</h4>
<p> Do not worry <img src="smiley.gif"
alt="Smiley face" align="top" width="32"
height="32"> be happy</p>

<h4> Image with align="left":</h4>
<p> Do not worry <img src="smiley.gif"
alt="Smiley face" align="left" width="32"
height="32"> be happy</p>

<h4> Image with align="right":</h4>
```

```
<p> Do not worry <img src="smiley.gif"
alt="Smiley face" align="right" width="32"
height="32"> be happy</p>

</body>
</html>
```

Note: *The img src code should contain the full path of the image on server along with an extension of the picture like, jpg, gif, png, etc.*

In some cases, the user turns off the images displayed in the browser for faster browsing. In such cases, we can make use of alt attribute of <img> tag. Even if the image is not displayed, the alternate text can be displayed and provide information to user about the image. Some browsers display alt text on mouse hover on the image. In this case, we may provide extra information about the image we can use the longdesc attribute. The longdesc attribute provides an URL to a document which is used as long description for Image. Allowing longdesc or disabling it totally depends on the browser.

Size and scaling
The size of the image can be defined using the height and width attribute of <img> tag. These attributes take values in pixels (to define the exact size of image) and percentage (to define the relative size of image according to browser window). Suppose we have a large, high resolution image, but we want to display it in small size. In this case, we can define the size attribute with pixel

values. The default value to set the height and width of image is always in pixels.

Example 6.3 – Image Size

```
<!DOCTYPE html>
<html>
<body>

<p> Full Size Image <img alt = "Full size image"
src="http://www.example.com/images/flower.jpg"
></p>
<p> Half Size Image <img alt = "Half-size image"
src=" http://www.example.com /images/flower.jpg"
width="90px"></p>

</body>
</html>
```

We should define both the height and width attributes for an image. Defining these attributes reserves the space for image when the page is loading. If both the attributes are not defined, the browser will be unaware of the image size and will change the page layout during loading until the image loads.

Image Maps

Image map facilitates mapping of some area of image into actions. There are two types of image maps: Client-side image and Server-side Image.

In Client-side, image maps are dependent upon the browser to load the image and provide the clickable region to user and perform the wanted action. Server-side image maps are dependent on browser only to inform the server where it the user clicked, and all processing is done by agent on Web server. Among the two, client-side image maps are generally used. They are fast, allow immediate action, and are supported by almost all the browsers. A client side image is defined within the contents of <map> tag and link to <img> tag along with <img> tag's usemap attribute.

Specifying clickable regions

To define an image map, a list of polygonal regions must be specified on image and should be stated in HTML document. There are three types of polygons:

1)   **Rectangle** - The rectangle (rect) defines a rectangular area by defining its coordinates (the four corners of rectangle).

2)   **Circle** – The circle defines its area by defining the coordinates of center of circle and its radius.

3)   **Free form polygon** – The free form polygon area is defined by the coordinates of each point of the polygon.

All coordinates of image map are defined with respect to the top-left corner of the image (effectively 0,0) and are measured in pixels.

Specifying regions using anchor tags

We can define regions using anchor tags by specifying its shape and coordinates of the attributes.

Example 6.4 – Image Maps

```
<!DOCTYPE html>
<html>
<body>

<p> Click on the Flower to watch it closer: </p>

<img src = "flower.gif" width = "145" height =
"126" alt = "Flower" usemap = "#flowermap">

<map name = "flowermap">
  <a shape = "rect" cords = "0,0,82,126" alt = "
brugmansia" href = "
http://www.example.com/brugmansia.htm">
  <a shape = "circle" cords = "90,58,3" alt = "
Fuchsia " href = "
http://www.example.com/fuchsia.htm">
  <a shape = "circle" cords = "124,58,8" alt = "
Impatiens " href = "
http://www.example.com/impatiens.htm">
</map>

</body>
</html>
```

Specifying regions using area tags

Regions can also be defined using <area> tags in place of anchors.

Example 6.5 – Area Tags

```
<!DOCTYPE html>
<html>
<body>

<p> Click on the Flower to watch it closer: </p>

<img src = " http://www.example.com/flower.gif"
width = "145" height = "126" alt = "Flower"
usemap = "#flowermap">

<map name = "flowermap">
  <area shape = "rect" cords = "0,0,82,126" alt = "
brugmansia " href = "
http://www.example.com/brugmansia.htm">
  <area shape = "circle" cords = "90,58,3" alt = "
Fuchsia " href = "
http://www.example.com/fuchsia.htm">
  <area shape = "circle" cords = "124,58,8" alt = "
Impatiens " href = "
http://www.example.com/impatiens.htm">
</map>

</body>
</html>
```

Even images can be hyperlinks.

To convert images into a hyperlink, just write HTML image code instead of the hyperlink text. Relative path (/images/smiley.gif) or absolute path (http://example.com/images/smiley.gif) can be provided as source to image.

Example 6.6 – Image Hyperlinks

```
<!DOCTYPE html>
<html>
<body>

<p> Create a link of an image:
<a href="htmltutorial.htm">
<img src=" http://www.example.com/smiley.gif"
alt="HTML tutorial" width="32"
height="32"></a></p>

<p> Image without border, but still a link:
<a href="
http://www.example.com/htmltutorial.htm ">
<img border="0" src="
http://www.example.com/smiley.gif" alt="HTML
tutorial" width="32" height="32"></a></p>

</body>
</html>
```

Chapter 7 – Lists and More Lists

In HTML, a list is just what it sounds like: it's a list of items. There are three main types of lists in HTML: ordered lists, unordered list, and definition lists. An ordered list will be numbered in a way, either with letters, numbers, roman numerals, or some other way defined by CSS. An unordered list is usually setup with bullets of some sort but contains no letters or numbers to represent a specific order. A definition list is a list that has a description of each grouping of items. These typically do not have bullets or any type of ordering.

Ordered List

An ordered list is defined by the <ol> tag. All of the items in the list are defined by the <li> tag. As stated earlier, all tags should be closed, but most browsers are smart enough to realize that when you open another list item <li> that you intended to close the previous one. Remember, ordered list have a defined order, either numbers, letters, or roman numerals.

See the example below to see how to create an ordered list. Also below is the sample output of an unformatted, generic ordered list.

Example 7.1 – Ordered List

```
<ol>
        <li>Item 1</li>
        <li>Item 2</li>
        <li>Item 3</li>
</ol>
```

Figure 7.1 – Ordered List

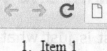

1. Item 1
2. Item 2
3. Item 3

Unordered List

An unordered list is a list that normally uses bullets to identify the items in the list. An unordered list can also be used to create menu items but styling the list using CSS. CSS can allow a list to be vertical or horizontal (think of a menu bar). CSS can change the colors, background, font, size, and wrapping or a list. The <ul> tag starts an unordered list. The list items use the same <li> tag that was used on an ordered list. Basically, if you have an ordered list and want to turn it into an unordered list, just change the 'ol' to a 'ul'. Below is a basic unformatted example of an unordered list.

Example 7.2 – Unordered List

```
<ul>
        <li>Item 1</li>
        <li>Item 2</li>
        <li>Item 3</li>
</ul>
```

Figure 7.2 – Unordered List

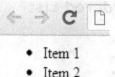

- Item 1
- Item 2
- Item 3

Definition List

The definition list is a little bit different from the ordered and unordered lists, but not that different. It's also the least used type of list. The dl tag starts the definition list. The <dt> tag defines or titles the item in the list. The <dd> tag describes the item in the list. Below is an example of using the definition list.

Example 7.3 – Definition List

```
<dl>
        <dt>The first item</dt>
            <dd>- item 1</dd>
        <dt>The second item</dt>
            <dd>- item 2</dd>
</dl>
```

Figure 7.3 – Definition List

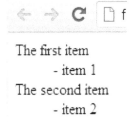

The first item
- item 1
The second item
- item 2

Nested List

You have the option in both ordered and unordered list to create "nested list." A nested list is just a list within a list. The browser is smart enough to understand that you are intending start a new list inside of an existing list when you do this. If you're nesting an ordered list, the counting of the list items will start over inside the nested list and resume once the list tag for the nested list is closed. The browser also indents a nested list to make them more attractive to the reader of the HTML document. See Example 7.4 and Figure 7.4 for an example of a nested ordered list and Example 7.5 and Figure 7.5 for an example of a nested unordered list. Also note that the bullets change for the nested unordered list.

Example 7.4 – Nested Ordered List

```
<p><strong>To Do List:</strong></p>
<ol>
        <li>Monday</li>
            <ol>
                <li>Cut grass</li>
                <li>Wash the car</li>
            </ol>
        <li>Tuesday</li>
            <ol>
                <li>Laundry</li>
                <li>Shopping</li>
            </ol>
</ol>
```

Figure 7.4 – Nested Ordered List

To Do List:

1. Monday
    1. Cut grass
    2. Wash the car
2. Tuesday
    1. Laundry
    2. Shopping

Example 7.5 – Nested Unordered List

```
<p><strong>To Do List:</strong></p>
<ul>
     <li>Monday</li>
          <ul>
               <li>Cut grass</li>
               <li>Wash the car</li>
          </ul>
     <li>Tuesday</li>
          <ul>
               <li>Laundry</li>
               <li>Shopping</li>
          </ul>
</ul>
```

Figure 7.5 –Nested Unordered List

To Do List:

- Monday
    - Cut grass
    - Wash the car
- Tuesday
    - Laundry
    - Shopping

Formatting Order Lists with "type"

Ordered List use numbers to maintain *order* by default, but this can be modified by using the "type" attribute. The "type" attribute can change the numbers to letters, both upper and lower cased, as well as roman numerals. See Example 7.6 and Figure 7.6 for an example.

Example 7.6 – Ordered List with "type"

```
<p><strong>Numbered :</strong></p>
<ol>
 <li>Cars</li>
 <li>Cars</li>
 <li>Trains</li>
</ol>

<p><strong>Letters :</strong></p>
<ol type="A">
 <li>Cars</li>
 <li>Cars</li>
 <li>Trains</li>
</ol>

<p><strong>Lowercase letters :</strong></p>
<ol type="a">
 <li>Cars</li>
 <li>Cars</li>
 <li>Trains</li>
</ol>

<p><strong>Roman numerals :</strong></p>
<ol type="I">
 <li>Cars</li>
 <li>Cars</li>
 <li>Trains</li>
</ol>

<p><strong>Lowercase roman numerals :</strong></p>
<ol type="i">
 <li>Cars</li>
 <li>Cars</li>
 <li>Trains</li>
</ol>
```

Figure 7.6 – Ordered List with "type"

Numbered :

1. Cars
2. Cars
3. Trains
4. Trains

Letters :

A. Cars
B. Cars
C. Trains
D. Trains

Lowercase letters :

a. Cars
b. Cars
c. Trains
d. Trains

Roman numerals :

I. Cars
II. Cars
III. Trains
IV. Trains

Lowercase roman numerals :

i. Cars
ii. Cars
iii. Trains
iv. Trains

Chapter 8 – It's all about Style

So far everything we've done has looked kind of bland and ugly in the browser. As you know, all successful webpages look good (except craigslist.org... there's always an exception to the rule). The way to make a webpage look good it is to implore the use of Cascading Style Sheets or CSS. CSS was designed as a way to separate the style from the HTML element to which it is applied. CSS can be used with html to completely change the appearance of a webpage. It can be used to dynamically show and hide content, change colors, fonts, images, and position of HTML elements. This book is about HTML, so we're not going to cover everything that there is to cover in CSS, but we are going to go over some of the basics.

There are three different forms in which CSS can be used to improve the appearance and functionality of a webpage. There are inline styles, embedded styles, and external style sheets. CSS is also applied to a webpage and acted upon by the browser in priority order with inline styles taking the highest priority, followed by embedded styles, and trailed by the most useful form, external style sheets.

Inline Styles

An inline style is a style element that is used within an HTML tag. It still uses a form of CSS, but it is wrapped directly in the HTML tag and is only applied to a single occurrence of the html element it is modifying. These are useful if you have an element that needs to have a unique style applied to it that won't be used anywhere else in the page. It can also be used to override an embedded style or external style sheet. An example of an inline style on a paragraph tag can be seen in Example 8.1 and Figure 8.1 below. Typically we don't recommend using inline styles on most websites. Inline styles are easy and quick to implement but can be difficult to maintain and update as the site grows.

Example 8.1 – Inline Style

```
<p style="color:white;font-family:courier;background-
color:gray;">This is white text</p>
<p style="color:gray;font-family:arial;">This is gray
text</p>
```

Figure 8.1 –Inline Style

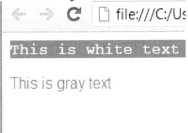

Embedded Styles

Embedded styles are pretty commonly implemented by What You See Is What You Get editors such as Microsoft Web Express. These styles control all of the occurrences of tags or classes within a particular page. These are also sometimes called Internal Style Sheets. These styles are defined inside of the <style> tag inside of the head section of your webpage. These are a bit easier to maintain going forward than inline styles; however, they still fall short of the maintainability that is achieved using external style sheets.

One option that you have when using embedded (as well as external) style sheets is that you can define ids and classes on certain tags or elements within your html. For example, let's say you want all of your hyperlinks on a page to be blue with no underlines.

Example 8.2 – Embedded Styles
```
<style>
        p       {
                margin-left:20px;
                font-family:arial;
                font-size: medium;
                }
        body    {
                background-image:url("images/bg.gif");
                }
</style>
```

External Styles
Linking to an external style sheet is the preferred way of styling a website. Linking to an external style sheet gives you the ability to change the style (look and appearance) on the entire site by just editing one file, instead of having to edit every page in the site. It also allows browsers to only need to download the style sheet once and cache it to improve performance and reduce bandwidth usage.

The link to a style sheet should be placed in the <head> tag of a webpage. This placement is done using the <link> tag. The standard elements of the link tag include a href attribute which points to the location of the CSS file, a type attribute that tells that the file being linked contains text and CSS, and a rel attribute that tells that the file is a stylesheet. An example of the link tag is as follows:

Example 8.3 – External Styles
```
<link rel="stylesheet" type="text/css" href="mystyle.css">
```

CSS Syntax
CSS is broken down into two main parts: a selector and a declaration. The selector tells which HTML element is going to be modified by the declaration. Each declaration is made up of two parts: a property and a value. The property identifies the style attribute that will be changed, and the value identifies that change that will take place for that attribute. All CSS declarations end in a semicolon. Like HTML, CSS ignores whitespace; however, we use whitespace to help make CSS more readable to the developer and designer. Below are two examples of the same CSS. Example 8.5 makes use of whitespace to make it easier to read than Example 8.4.

Example 8.4 – Minified Styles

```
p{margin-left:20px;font-family:arial;font-size:
medium;}body{background-image:url("images/bg.gif");}
```

Example 8.5 – Use of Whitespace in Styles

```
p       {
        margin-left:20px;
        font-family:arial;
        font-size: medium;
        }
body    {
        background-image:url("images/bg.gif");
        }
```

Both produce the same result, but it's pretty clear that Example 8.5 is easier to see what's going on.

Like HTML, CSS can have comments to omit parts of code so that the browser will ignore it. These comments are also used to make notes for the designers/developers to refer back to at later dates. Comments in CSS begin with "/*" and end with "*/", see Example 8.6.

Example 8.6 – Comments

```
/* Comment for the body */
Body { background-image:url("images/bg.gif");
/* OLD Body
Body { background-image:url("images/bg-old.gif");
/*
```

CSS is the preferred way of styling a website. With the use of a linked (external) style sheet, the task of formatting a website can be made much simpler than legacy code of HTML styles. Appendix C includes a CSS reference guide with common CSS selectors and declarations. To learn more about CSS, visit http://www.whatscss.com.

Chapter 9 – Frames and Tables

The concept of a "Frame" page in HTML is pretty much dead. You shouldn't use frame pages. They don't work for SEO and are just an older way of doing things. iFrames on the other hand are still acceptable and can be very useful.

What is an Iframe?

In a browser window, the section in which a web page loads is known as frame. Inline frame allows smaller sections of content to be included in container with scroll bar within the large document. Hence name Inline Frame. We can also use the normal frameset to create small scrolling regions but the using regular frameset hampers the layout. Inline frames can be created using <iframe> tag and use the following format:

Example 9.1 - iFrame
<iframe scr="url_of_content"></iframe>

The attributes of <iframe> tag are:

1) **Align**: This attribute is used for aligning the frame according to the neighboring text. The possible values of align attributes are left, right, top, middle, and bottom.

2) **Frameborder**: This attribute defines whether the frame should be surrounded by a visible border or not. The possible values of a frameborder attribute are 0 or 1. 0 indicates no border and 1 indicate border. The default value is 1.

3) **Height**: This attribute defines the height of the frame. The value of this attribute is in pixels %.

4) **Longdesc**: This attribute defines a URL to a document containing the long description of frame. The value of the Longdesc attribute is URL of the document.

5) **Marginheight**: This attribute set the margin of the frame (internal top and bottom margin). The value of marginheight is in pixels.

6) **Marginwidth**: This attribute set the internal left and right margin of the frame. The value of marginwidth is in pixels.

7) **Name**: This attribute defines the name of frame which can be used for accessing the frame and scripting. The value of this attribute is name_of_frame.

8) **Scrolling**: This attribute defines whether the frame should have scrollbars or not. The possible values of scrolling attribute is yes, no, and auto. Auto is the default value.

9) **Src**: This attribute used to display the URL of the content in frame. The value of scr attribute is the URL of the content.

10) **Width**: This attribute defines the width of the frame. The value of this attribute is pixels%.

We can use various attributes in <iframe> tag to achieve the desire frame layout.

The only drawback of inline frames is that it is supported by few browsers, so it is advisable to use the inline frame only if we know that audience will use the browsers that are compatible with inline frames.

Example 9.2 - Simple inline frame

```
<!DOCTYPE html>
<html>
<body>

<iframe src="example_iframe.htm" width="300"
height="300"></iframe>

<p>Some browsers don't support iframes.</p>
<p>If they don't, the iframe will not be
visible.</p>

</body>
</html>
```

John Rouda

Figure 9.1 – Simple Inline Frame

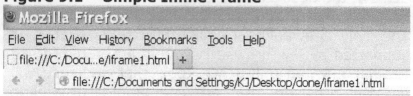

Some browsers don't support iframes.

If they don't, the iframe will not be visible.

Example 9.3 - Inline frame with no border

```
<!DOCTYPE html>
<html>
<body>

<iframe src="example_iframe.htm"
frameborder="0"></iframe>

<p>Some older browsers don't support
iframes.</p>
```

```
<p>If they don't, the iframe will not be
visible.</p>


</body>
</html>
```

Example 9.2 Inline frame with no border

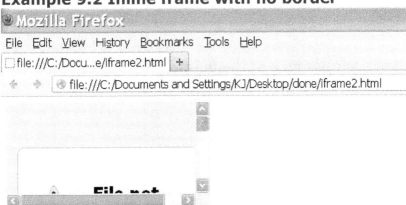

Some older browsers don't support iframes.

If they don't, the iframe will not be visible.

Example 9.4 - Target frame for link

```
<!DOCTYPE html>
<html>
<body>

<iframe src="example_iframe.htm"
name="iframe_a"></iframe>
<p><a href="http://www.example.com"
target="iframe_a">example.com</a></p>

<p><b>Note:</b> Because the target of the link
matches the name of the iframe, the link will open
in the iframe.</p>

</body>
</html>
```

Figure 9.3 - Target frame for link

example.com

Note: Because the target of the link matches the name of the iframe, the link will open in the iframe

Div Element

In HTML, div element acts like a container that wraps page elements and divides the HTML document into several parts. When used with style sheets, div elements can design a document's layout. Div element has replaced the old way of designing layout with tables to provide division of content.

Div Elements Attributes:

1) Identifier <id>: This attribute defines a identifier to the element. Identifier must have unique value which can be used in referring that element.
2) Class: This attribute denotes a class name to container element. It can be used along with style sheets and informs the browser about the corresponding element.
3) Style: An name indicates this element provide better presentation to the div element. It can define text color, font-size, background color, etc.

Example 9.5 – Div Elements

```
<!DOCTYPE html>
<html>
<body>

<div style="background-color:grey;text-align:center">
```

```
  <p>Navigation bar</p>
</div>
<div style="border:1px solid black">
<marquee>  <p>Picture slider</p> </marquee>
</div>

<div style="color:#0000FF;text-align:center">
<h3>Heading in a div element</h3>
<p>Your text can display here. </p> </div>

<div style="background-color:grey;text-
align:center">
  <p>Footer</p>


</div>

</body>
</html>
```

Figure 9.4 – Div Elements

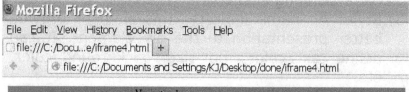

A table is exactly what it sounds like, especially if you're familiar with a table in MS Word. It is a combination of rows and columns, and their intersection is known as a cell. In a cell, we can write text, insert images, or create tables too.

Creating a table

The table is created using a <table> tag. Once the table is defined using the <table> tag, we can include table's row tag <tr> within each <tr> tag we can include table data <td> tag. <td> tag is used to define cells in table. The number of columns in a table is equal to the highest number of <td> in a row. By default, a table is displayed without a border. To display the border of the table, we can use border attribute.

Example 9.6 - Table

```
<!DOCTYPE html>
<html>
<body>

<h3>Table with one column</h3>
<table border="1">
<tr>
  <td>222</td>
</tr>
</table>

<h3>Table with one row and two columns:</h3>
<table border="1">
<tr>
```

```
 <td>111</td>
 <td>444</td>
 </tr>
</table>

<h3>Table with two rows and two columns:</h3>
<table border="1">
<tr>
  <td>666</td>
  <td>888</td>
</tr>
<tr>
  <td>333</td>
  <td>123</td>
</tr>

</table>
</body>
</html>
```

Figure 9.5 – Table

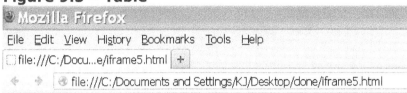

In the above example, we can also add header to table known as <th> tag. By default, the text in <th> tag is displayed in bold and centered.

Example 9.7 – Table Header:

```
<!DOCTYPE html>
<html>
<body>

<h3> Example of table headers </h3>
<table border="1">
<tr>
  <th> Name</th>
  <th> Roll no</th>
```

```
</tr>
<tr>
 <td> AAA</td>
 <td> 1</td>

</tr>
</table>

<h3> Vertical headers: </h3>
<table border="1">
<tr>
 <th> First Name: </th>
 <td> AAA</td>
</tr>
<tr>
 <th> Address: </th>
 <td> ABC bungalow, xyz street </td>
</tr>
<tr>
 <th> Telephone: </th>
 <td> 555 77 855 </td>
</tr>
</table>

</body>
</html>
```

Figure 9.6 – Table Header

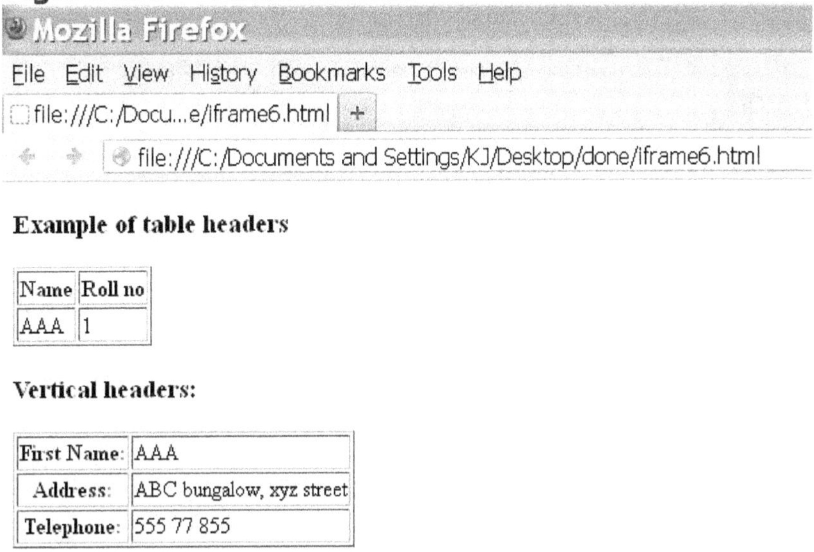

We can add a caption to the table using <caption> tag inside the <table> tag

Defining table size

The table accommodates itself according to its highest entries in that row or column. Whenever a cell is added or deleted, the table size expands and compresses accordingly. Sometimes we need to define table size for constraining the table or filling a large space.

Defining the width attribute inside <table> tag, we can manually set the table size. The value of the width attribute can either be in pixels or percentage of enclose object.

Defining the value of width in percentage allows the table to resize itself dynamically according to the size of container. If we want a table to be fixed in size, we must define width in pixels.

<table width=100%>
<table width=900px>

We can also align the elements in the table using align attribute in <table> tag. The possible values of align attribute can be left, right, and center.

Example 9.8 – Table Alignment

```
<!DOCTYPE html>
<html>
<body>

<p>Table with cellspacing:</p>
<table border="1" width="300" cellspacing="10">
   <tr>
   <th>First Name</th>
   <th>number</th>
  </tr>
  <tr>
   <td>AAA</td>
   <td>001</td>
  </tr>
</table>
</body>
</html>
```

Figure 9.7

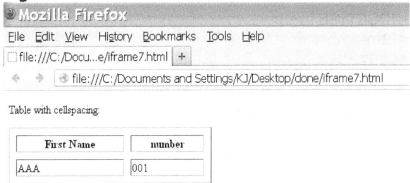

Padding and cell spacing

Space between the cells is known as cell spacing. Spacing between cell border and its contents is known as cell padding. Cell spacing can be obtained by defining the cell spacing attribute either in percentage or in pixels. The browser uses half of the defined value for each side of cell if the value is defined in percentage.

Example 9.9 – Cell spacing and cell padding

```
<!DOCTYPE html>
<html>
<body>

<p>Table with cellspacing:</p>
<table border="1" cellspacing="10">
  <tr>
    <th>Roll number</th>
    <th>Name</th>
  </tr>
  <tr>
    <td>001</td>
    <td>AAA</td>
  </tr>
</table>

<p>Table with cellpadding:</p>
<table border="1" cellpadding="10">
  <tr>
    <th>Roll number</th>
    <th>Name</th>
  </tr>
  <tr>
    <td>001</td>
    <td>AAA</td>
  </tr>
</table>

</body>
</html>
```

Figure 9.8 - Cell spacing and cell padding

Table Rows

As discussed earlier to create a row in the table we use <tr> tag. The row is divided into different cells using<td> or <th>. The <tr> tag has some attributes. Those are align, char, charoff, and valign.

1) **Align**: This attribute set the horizontal alignment of text in a row. The possible values of align are right, left, center, and justify.
2) **Char**: This attribute defines the alignment character to use along char alignment.
3) **Charoff**: This attribute outlines the offset from alignment character to align data.

4) **Valign**: This attribute sets the vertical alignment of data in row.

Example 9.10 - Align in row

```
<!DOCTYPE html>
<html>
<body>

<table width="100%" border="1">
  <tr align="center">
   <th>Roll number</th>
    <th>Name</th>

  </tr>
  <tr align="center">
     <td>001</td>
    <td>AAA</td>

  </tr>
</table>
</body>
</html>
```

Figure 9.9 - Align in row

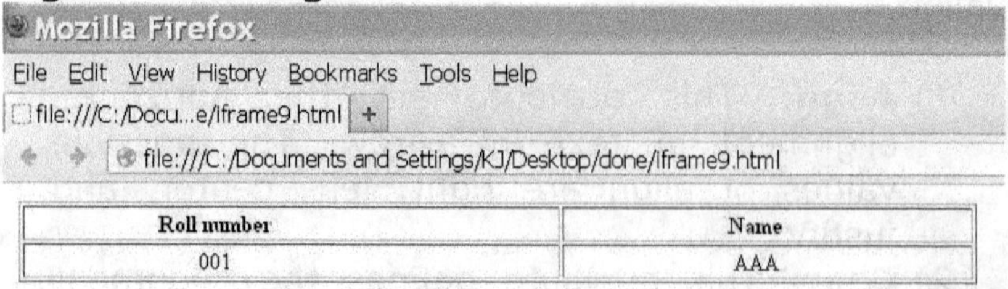

Example 9.11 - valign

```
<!DOCTYPE html>
<html>
<body>

<table border="1" style="height:200px">
  <tr valign="middle">
     <th>Roll number</th>
   <th>Name</th>

  </tr>
  <tr valign="bottom">
      <td>001</td>
   <td>AAA</td>

  </tr>
  <tr valign="baseline">
    <td>001</td>
   <td>AAA</td>

  </tr>
</table>
</body>
</html>
```

Figure 9.10 – valign

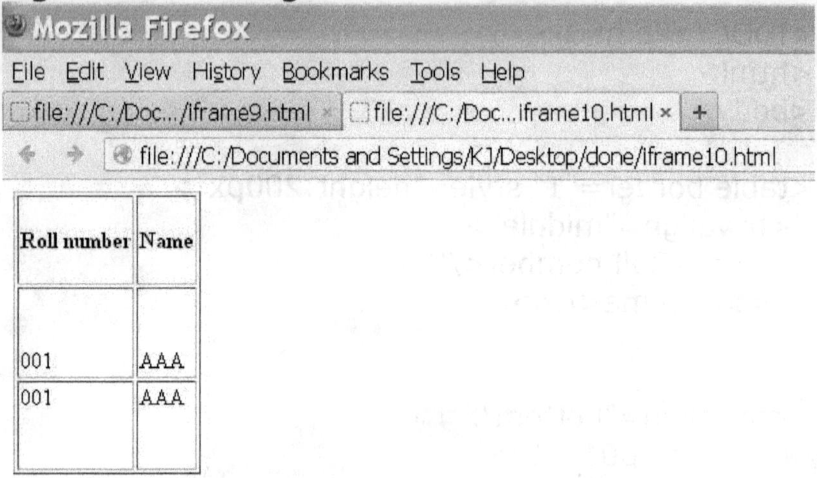

Merging Table cells

In a table, each and every cell is the same size; we can't change the individual size of the cell. We can merge the cell, like multiple cells of one row or column into a single cell.

To merge adjacent cells of a cell into one cell, we use colspan attribute in <td> and specify the number to columns to be merged (span).

<td colspan="4">

To merge the adjacent cell below a cell into one cell, we use rowspan attribute and define the number of rows to be merged.

<td rowspan="3">

Example 9.12 - Merge

```
<!DOCTYPE html>
<html>
<body>


<table border="1">
  <tr>
    <td colspan="2" rowspan="2"> Survey Results </td>
    <td colspan="3">Age</td>
  </tr>
  <tr>
    <td>12 to 20</td>
    <td>20 to 40</td>
    <td>Over 40</td>
  </tr>
  <tr>
    <td rowspan="3"> "What type of TV shows do u like" </td>
    <td>Adventurous TV shows</td>
    <td>25%</td>
    <td>50%</td>
    <td>25%</td>
  </tr>
  <tr>
    <td>Comedy TV shows</td>
```

```
      <td>25%</td>
      <td>50%</td>
      <td>25%</td>
   </tr>
   <tr>
      <td>Thriller TV Shows</td>
      <td>25%</td>
      <td>50%</td>
      <td>25%</td>
   </tr>
</table>
```

Figure 9.11 – Merge

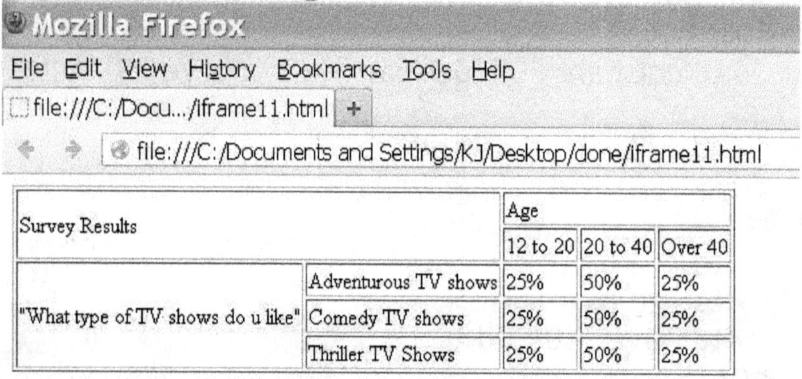

Survey Results		Age		
		12 to 20	20 to 40	Over 40
"What type of TV shows do u like"	Adventurous TV shows	25%	50%	25%
	Comedy TV shows	25%	50%	25%
	Thriller TV Shows	25%	50%	25%

Chapter 10 – Simple Forms

HTML forms allocate different controls to browser which facilitates the user to enter their data with ease. Further, this data is sent by browser to a server. The form is composed of various input elements like text fields, radio-buttons, textarea, checkbox, fieldset, submit buttons, and many others.

Let's have a quick look at an example of form.

Example 10.1 - Form

```
<!DOCTYPEHTMLPUBLIC"-
//W3C//DTDHTML4.01//EN"
"http://www.w3.org/TR/html4/strict.dtd">
<html>
<head>
<title> A Simple Form </title>
</head>
<body>
<form action="formhandler.php" method="post">
<table cellspacing="30">
<tr> <td>
<!--Textboxes-->

<p> <label for = "fname" >First Name: </label>
<input type = "text" name = "fname" id = "fname"
size="30"> <br>
<label for = "lname"> Last Name: </label>
<input type = "text" name = "lname" id="lname"
size="30">
</p>
                <!—Text area-->
```

```
<p> <label for="address"> Address: </label>
<br>
<textarea name="address" id="address" cols=30
rows=4> </textarea>
</p>                <!--Password-->
<p> <label for="password"> Password: </label>
<input type = "password" name = "password"
id="password" size="30">
</p>
</td>
<td>

          <!—Select list-->
<p> <label for="subject"> Subject <br> interested
in ? </label> <br>
<select name="sub[]"id="subject"
multiple="multiple"
size="4">
<option id="Math"> Mathematics
<option id="Comp"> Computer
<option id="Bio"> Biology
<option id="Chem">Chemistry
<option id="Phy">Physics
<option id="Ele">Electronics
</select>
</p>
          <!--Checkboxes-->
<fieldset>
<legend> Contact me via:</legend>
<p> <input type="checkbox" name="email"
id="email" checked>
<label for="email"> Email </label> <br>
<input type="checkbox" name="postal"
id="postal">
<label for="postal">Postal Address</label></p>
```

```
</fieldset>

</td>
</tr>
<tr>
<td>

<!—Radio buttons-->
<fieldset>
<p> In which format do you want the tutorials</p>
<legend> </legend>
<p><input type="radio" name="format"
value="PDF" id="formatPDF">
<label for = " formatPDF" > PDF </label><br>
<input type = "radio" name = "format"
value="word" id=" formatword">
<label for = "formatword"> Word </label> <br>

</fieldset>

</td>
<td>

</td>

<td>
<!—Submit and Reset buttons-->
<p>
<input type="submit" value="submit">
<input type ="reset" value="clear">

</p>
<!--Button-->
<p>
```

```
<input type ="button" name ="Leave"
value="Leave site!">
</p>
</td>
</tr>
</table>
</form>
</body>
</html>
```

Figure 10.1 – Form

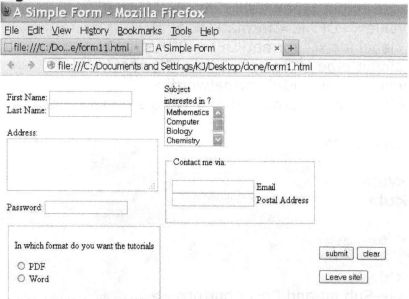

Let us discuss the HTML form in detail.

We can create a basic form by using a
<form> tag. <form> tag needs one basic attribute
that is a "method." The method attribute defines

what action will take place once the form is submitted. <form> tag ends with a closing </form> tag.

Example 10.2.1 – Method attribute

```
<form method="post">
...
</form>
```

Almost every form uses method with post value. This means the data entered by the user will be passed to the server where server side code will store them in database. The post method sends encoded data to the server in such a way that user cannot see it. The other value to method attribute is get. In get, the data is attached to URL and sends to the server. The user can easily view the data in the URL. This is not safe as anyone can sniff and modify the data.

Other attributes of form are accept, accept-charset, enctype, name, and target.

Field Labels

The <label> tag defines labels for form inputs. Many users depend on the layout of the form to decide which labels should be used with which fields.

Example 10.2.2 –Field Labels

```
<!DOCTYPE html>
<html>
<body>

<p>Marital status</p>

<form action="demo_form.php">
  <label for="married">Married</label>
  <input type="radio" name="status" id="married"
value="married"><br>
  <label for="unmarried">Single</label>
  <input type="radio" name="status" id="single"
value="single"><br><br>
  <input type="submit" value="submit">
</form>

</body>
</html>
```

Figure 10.2 – Field Labels

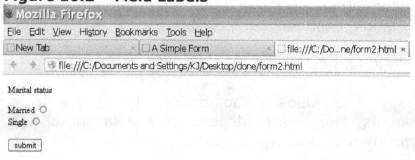

Creating a text box

Text box is used commonly for entering data such as name, address, comments, etc. There are two types of text box: regular text box (Single line) and text areas (multi-lines).

Example 10.3 – Text Inputs

```
<!DOCTYPE html>
<html>
<body>
<form>

First name: <input type="text"
name="firstname"><br>
Phone number: <input type="text"
name="phonenumber">

<p> Please type your message</p>
<textarea rows="10" cols="30">
</textarea>
</form>

</body>
</html>
```

Figure 10.3 – Text Inputs

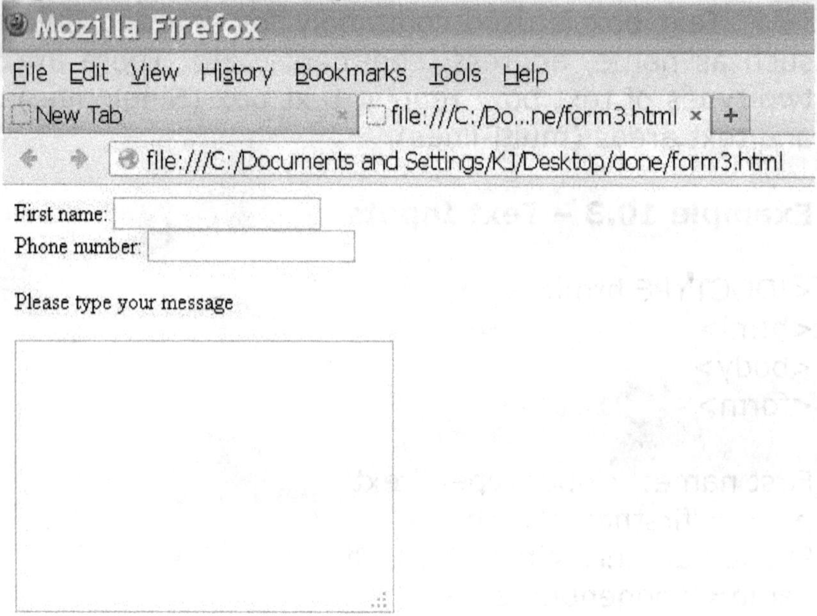

We can set the width of a text box with size attribute. The default width is 20 pixels. We can also set the maximum length for text string that the user can enter into text box. When the user exceeds the maximum number of characters, the text box does not accept input.

Example 10.4 – Text Boxes

```
<!DOCTYPE html>
<html>
<body>

<form>
First name: <input type="text"
name="firstname"><br>
Phone number: <input type="text"
name="phonenumber">

<p> Please type your message</p>
<input type="text" name="message" size="30"
maxlength="100">

</form>
</body>
</html>
```

Figure 10.4 – Text Boxes

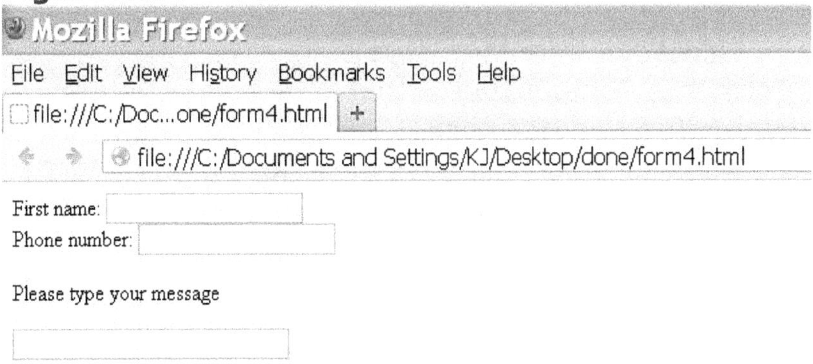

We can create a text area using <textarea> tag along with row attribute that defines number of text lines that text box can contain and column attribute that defines number of characters (each character represents a single column). The default number of characters is 40.

Please do not confuse the column attribute and maxlength. The column attribute defines size of text area and maxlength attribute sets the limit of character the user can enter as input to text area.

Password input box is a type of textbox which displays the input data in form of asterisks or disc.

Example 10.5 – Password Fields

```
<!DOCTYPE html>
<html>
<body>

<form>
<p> Already a member </p>
First name: <input type="text"
name="firstname"><br>
Customer number: <input type="text"
name="customernumber"><br>
<p>Password:<input type="password"
name="password" value=""
size="20" maxlength="20"></p>

</form>
</body>
</html>
```

Figure 10.5 – Password Fields

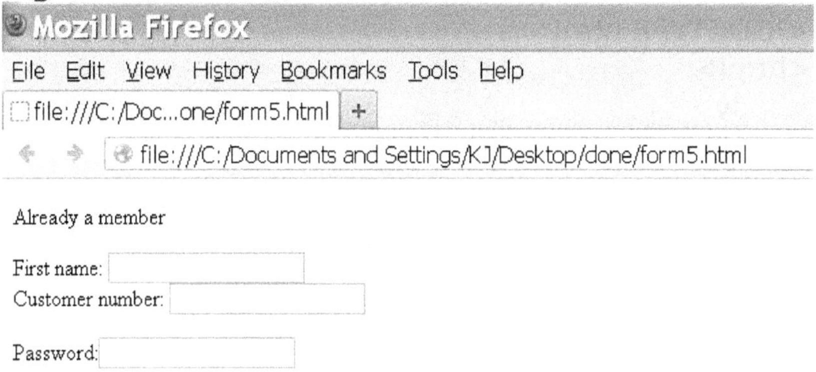

Making submit or reset button

In the above example, we have entered the data in all the entries, but we are unable to send it to the server. This is because the submit button was not available, so let's create one.

Submit refers to the action perform by the button and not just the wording. By default, we use the text "submit" on the button, but it can also be modified. The same is the case with the reset button; we can change its text on the button.

Example 10.6 - Buttons

```
<!DOCTYPE html>
<html>
<body>

<form>
<p> Already a member </p>
First name: <input type="text"
name="firstname"><br>
Customer number: <input type="text"
name="customernumber"><br>
<p>Password:<input type="password"
name="password" value=""
size="20" maxlength="20"></p>

  <input type="submit" value="submit">
  <input type="reset" value="clear">

</form>
</body>
</html>
```

Figure 10.6 – Buttons

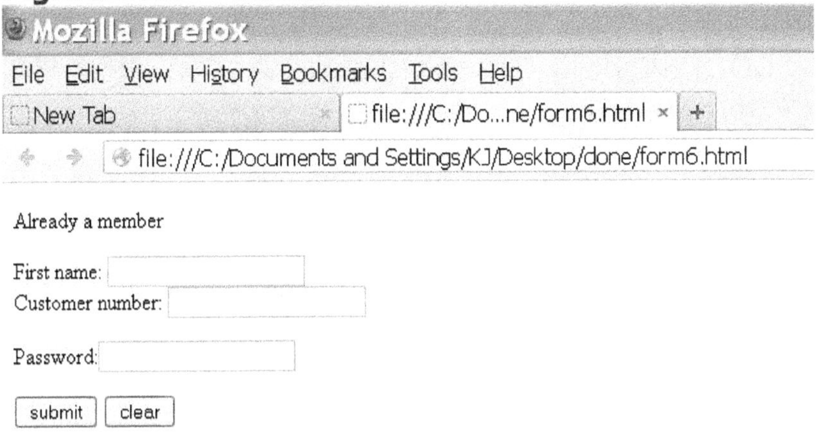

Creating Radio Buttons

Radio button are group of round small buttons that let the user to select any one option from the group. To create radio buttons use type="radio" attribute with <input> tag.
<input type="radio" name="color" id="red" value= "red" >

The value attribute tells us what value should be passed to the handler if the button is selected. Value attribute should be unique among the group of buttons.

In some cases, we need to select at least one option among all. In such a case, users prefer to pre-select an option. To select a default value, we can use checked attribute in <input> tag.

Example 10.7 – Radio Buttons

```
<!DOCTYPE html>
<html>
<body>
<form>
<p>Select Favorite Color</p>

  <input type="radio" name="color" id="Red"
value="Red"> Red <br>
  <input type="radio" name=" color " id="Blue"
value="Blue"> Blue <br>
  <input type="radio" name=" color " id="Green"
value=" Green "> Green <br>
  <input type="radio" name=" color " id="Black"
value=" Black "> Black <br>
  <input type="radio" name=" color " id="Pink"
value="Pink"> Pink <br>
  <input type="radio" name=" color "
id="Turquoise" value=" Turquoise "> Turquoise
<br> <br>
  <input type="submit" value="submit">
</form>

</body>
</html>
```

Figure 10.7 – Radio Buttons

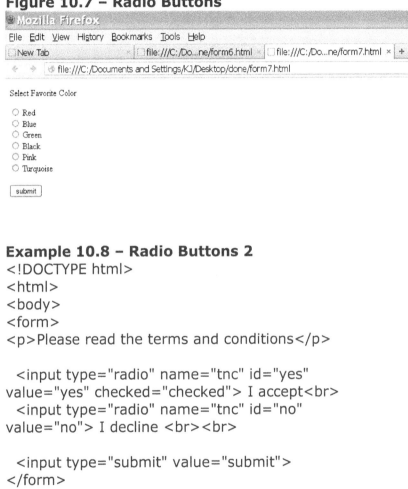

Example 10.8 – Radio Buttons 2

```
<!DOCTYPE html>
<html>
<body>
<form>
<p>Please read the terms and conditions</p>

  <input type="radio" name="tnc" id="yes"
value="yes" checked="checked"> I accept<br>
  <input type="radio" name="tnc" id="no"
value="no"> I decline <br><br>

  <input type="submit" value="submit">
</form>

</body>
</html>
```

Figure 10.8 – Radio Buttons 2

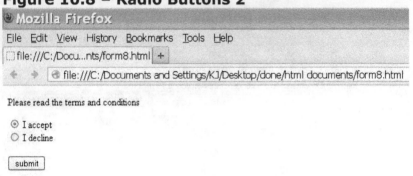

Creating Check boxes

As name indicates, check boxes are small square boxes which when selected displays a checkmark. We use check marks where we need multi-selections. To create a checkbox, we use type="checkbox" attribute along with <input> tag.
<input type="checkbox" name="hobbies">

The value of the selected button is on by default. If we want to modify the value, we can do it in the following way:

<input type="checkbox" name="hobbies"
        value="coin collection">

In some cases, we need to select at least one option among all. In this case, users prefer to pre-select an option. To select a default value, we can use checked attribute in <input> tag.

Example 10.9 – Check Boxes

```
<!DOCTYPE html>
<html>
<body>
<form>
<p>Select Your Hobbies</p>

  <input type="checkbox" name="hobby"
id="reading" value="Reading"> Reading <br>
  <input type="checkbox" name="hobby"
id="writing" value=" writing "> writing <br>
  <input type="checkbox" name="hobby"
id="singing" value=" singing "> singing <br>
  <input type="checkbox" name="hobby"
id="dancing" value=" dancing "> dancing <br>
<br> <br>
  <input type="submit" value="submit">
</form>

</body>
</html>
```

Figure 10.9 – Check Boxes

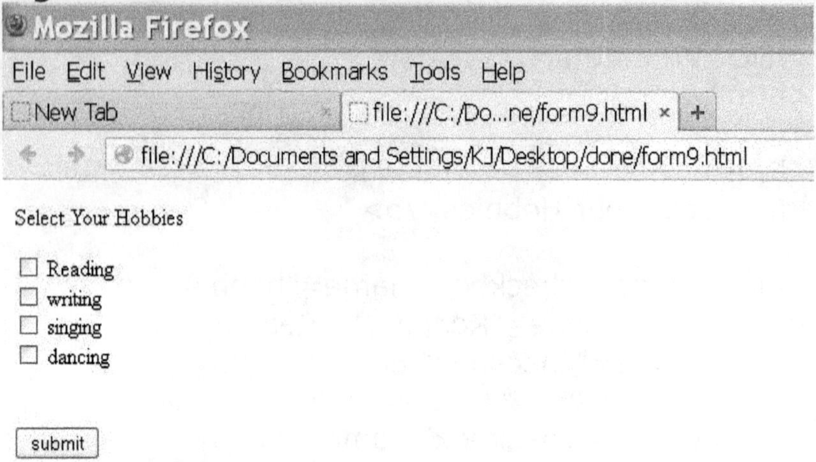

Mozilla Firefox

File Edit View History Bookmarks Tools Help

New Tab file:///C:/Do...ne/form9.html × +

file:///C:/Documents and Settings/KJ/Desktop/done/form9.html

Select Your Hobbies

☐ Reading
☐ writing
☐ singing
☐ dancing

[submit]

Drop Down List

The drop down list is created using the <select> element. As the name indicates, only one item can be seen with the small down arrow icon on one side. When the icon is clicked, the list is displayed in drop down manner. A drop down list consist of two tags: a <select> tag and an <option> tag.

The <select> tag defines the elements of drop down list, and the <option> tag denotes single selection. Each item that should appear in the drop down list should start with an opening <option> tag and should end with closing</option> tag. The first item in list will be default item that appears in text area of drop down list.

Example 10.10 – Drop Down Lists

```
<!DOCTYPE html>
<html>
<body>
<form>
 <p>Select subjects</p>
<select>
 <option
value="mathematics">mathematics</option>
  <option value="science">science</option>
  <option value="history">history</option>
  <option value="geography">geography</option>
</select>
<br><br>
  <input type="submit" value="submit">
</form>
</body>
</html>
```

We can also select multiple items. We need to add multiple in the <option> tag

Figure 10.10 – Drop Down Lists

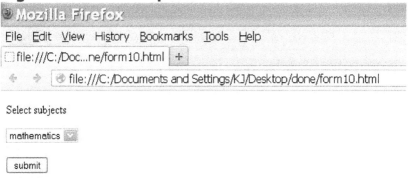

Example 10.11 - Multiple selection

```
<!DOCTYPE html>
<html>
<body>
<form>
 <p>Select flowers for your bouquet</p>
<select name="flowers" multiple>
  <option value="rose">rose</option>
  <option value="lily">lily</option>
  <option value="fuchsia">fuchsia</option>
  <option
value="chrysanthemum">chrysanthemum</option
>
</select>
<br><br>
  <input type="submit" value="submit">
</form>
</body>
</html>
```

Figure 10.11 - Multiple selection

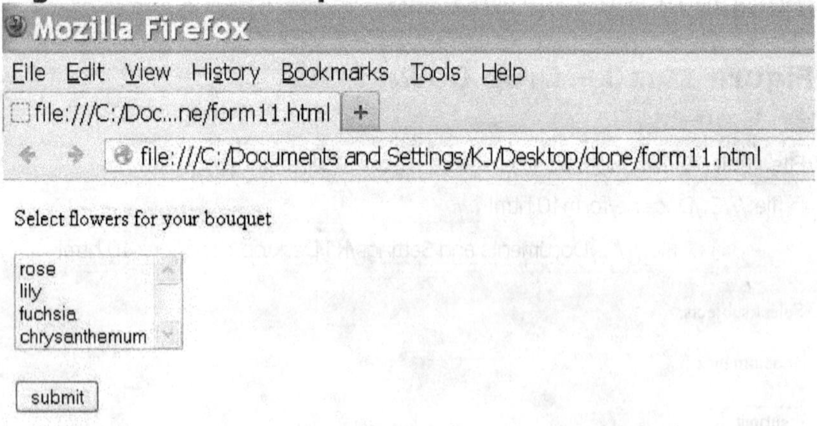

Mozilla Firefox

File   Edit   View   History   Bookmarks   Tools   Help

file:///C:/Doc...ne/form11.html   +

file:///C:/Documents and Settings/KJ/Desktop/done/form11.html

Select flowers for your bouquet

rose
lily
fuchsia
chrysanthemum

submit

List Boxes

List Boxes allow users to select multiple items from a list. List boxes can be displayed as a pull-down list or each and every element is evident. To create a list box, we use <select> and <option> tag. The <select> tag acts as a container for list box while the <option> tag specifies the items of the list. The <optgroup> tag is optional; it encapsulates all the items which should be in one group.

Example 10.12 – List Boxes

```
<!DOCTYPE html>
<html>
<body>
<form>
<p>Select the online games you want to play</p>
<select name="games" size="8"
multiple="multiple">
<optgroup label="Paid">
<option>Game of life
<option>Speed Rovers
</optgroup>
<optgroup label="Free"
<option>NFS
<option>Biker's den
<option>Mario
</optgroup>
</select>
<input type="submit" value="submit">
</form>
</body>
</html>
```

Figure 10.12 - List Boxes

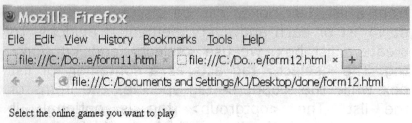

Select the online games you want to play

 submit

Make a Button.

Occasionally, we might need custom buttons on our form. To create a button, use button attribute in <input> tag. A button follows the following format:

```
<input type="button" name="buy_now"
          value="buy_now">
```

Example 10.3 – Making Buttons

```
<!DOCTYPE html>
<html>
<body>

<form action="">
<input type="button" value="buy now!">
</form>

</body>
</html>
```

Figure 10.13 – Making Buttons

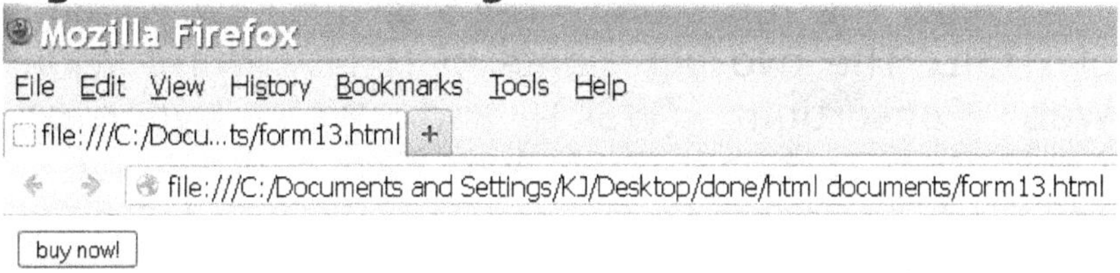

Chapter 11 – HTML5

Now the fun stuff. HTML5 is the new version of HTML. The two big giants of HTML, World Wide Web Consortium (W3C) and Web Hypertext Application Technology Working Group (WHATWG), are working together to improve HTML5. HTML5's new advance features are based on HTML, CSS, DOM, and JavaScript. HTML5 is so advanced and self-sufficient that now there is no need to use Flash or Silverlight because everything is present in the code. There are remarkable changes in HTML5 which includes new doctype, new structural elements, charset, canvas, and various API's like timed media playback, drag-and-drop, microdata, and geolocation.

Let's have a detailed look at HTML5

DOCTYPE

DOCTYPE stands for "Document Type Definition" which is the first line of an HTML page. DOCTYPE informs the browser about the type of document and how it should be processed. HTML5 DOCTYPE is converted into simpler versions. The DTD and other attributes are omitted, so now DOCTYPE is not case sensitive.

New Elements in HTML5

Section Element

As its name indicates, section element represents an application section.

Article Element
Article represents a complete or independent page or site that can be used again and again. Articles can also be nested with the inner article related to the content of the outer article.

Main Element
The main element acts as a container for the content of other elements, but only one main element is allowed.

Aside Element
Aside represents content that is slightly related to the page.

Header Element
The header element represents the group of navigation aids.

Footer Element
The footer element represents a footer which contains information about author and other links etc.

Nav Element
It represents a special place in document allocated for navigation.

Video and Audio Element
Video is used for displaying videos in webpage and audio is for listening to audio files in webpage. Some attributes of video element are autoplay, play, and pause.

Progress
The progress element shows the status of completion of task like downloading, uploading, and file transfer.

Meter
Meter is used to measure the disk usage.

Time
Time represents date and time.

Dialog:
Dialog shows a dialog window – i.e. a little box on the screen.

Ruby, rt, rp
Ruby, rt, rp allows ruby language annotations.

Canvas
Canvas allows drawing graphics via scripting.

Menuitem
Menuitem represents a command that invokes popup menu.

Input Elements
In HTML5, there are new input element types. The new input type attribute can have following values. These were created primarily for some specific advantages when access the web on a smart phone.

Tel

Tel enables control in editing a telephone number.

Search

Search, as name indicates, it is used for searching the text.

Url

Url enables control in editing an absolute URL.

Email

Email enables control in editing an email address.

datetime

Datetime sets the value of an element to a string representing the global date and time.

Date

Date enables control to set the value of an element to a string representing specific date.

Month

Month changes the value of an element to a string representing a specific month.

Week

Week allows an element to be set to a specific week.

Datetime-local

Datetime-local sets an element to the local date and time without time zone offset information.

Number

Number programs an element to represent a number.

Color

Color represents a color-well control to set value to string representing a simple color.

Form Elements in HTML5

Name input field

Names are always in character; they do not contain numbers or special characters, so input field should accept only characters. In HTML5, an alternative is given to browser to validate input field. As soon as the user enters any invalid input character on the name field, he/she will be alerted by a display message.

```
<input type="name" />
```

Username input field

Username element validates a username on the browser itself.

```
<input type="text" name="username"
pattern="^[a-zA-Z&393;&391;a-zA-Z0-
9&393;{1,10}$"/>
```

Password input field

Password element validates the password inputted by the user on the browser. Password should not be any scripts or language code.

```
<input type="password" name="password"
accept="text/plain" align="middle" />
```

Date input field

Date is a generic tag found on every form or webpages. We can define a range under which this date tag will be accepted input.

```
<input type="submit" name="Submit"
value="submit" />
```

Email Validation

HTML5 can validate email input from the browser itself without using any JavaScript code.

```
< input type="email"/>
```

URL element

HTML5 introduced a tag for URL validation.

```
<input type="URL"/>
```

There are a few changes in the attributes as well. Let's have a look.

Accept attribute

In accept attribute, the values audio/*, video/* and image/* are allowed.

Accesskey attribute

The accesskey attribute allows multiple characters to be defined.

Action attribute

The action attribute is not allowed to have an empty URL.

Colspan attribute

The colspan attribute on <td> and <th> must be greater than zero.

Cords attribute

The cords attribute cannot have a percentage value of the radius.

Data attribute

The data attribute cannot be relative to the codebase attribute.

Defer attribute

The defer attribute can explicitly execute the script once the page has finished parsing.

Dir attribute

The auto value is valid in dir global attribute.

Width and height attributes

The width and height attributes on object, image, and iframes are not allowed to contain percentages.

Href attribute

The href attribute in a link cannot have an empty URL. The href attribute is allowed to have a relative URL.

Target attribute

The target attribute of the anchor and area elements can be used with iframe.

The following elements are removed from HTML because their function can be handled by CSS:

1) basefont
2) big
3) center
4) font
5) strike
6) tt

For more CSS information visit
http://www.whatscss.com

The following elements are removed from HTML because they are efficient for reusability:

1) frame
2) frameset
3) noframes

The following elements are removed from HTML they are not used regularly and their function can be performed by other elements:

1) acronym because it creates lot of confusion.
2) applet
3) isindex
4) dir

Obsolete Attributes

HTML5 has advice on what you can use instead.

1) Use rev and charset attributes on link and <a>.
2) Use shape and coords attributes on <a>.
3) Use longdesc attribute on img and iframe.
4) Use target attribute on link.
5) Use name attribute on img.
6) Use profile attribute on head.
7) Use nohref attribute on area.
8) Use axis attribute on td and th
9) Use abbr and scope attribute on td
10)   Use summary attribute on table.

Obsolete Attributes

1) Do not use alink , vlink , text, and link attributes on body.
2) Do not use background on body.
3) Do not use bgcolor attribute on table, tr, th, body and td.
4) Do not use cellpadding on table.
5) Do not use cellspacing on table.
6) Do not use clear attribute on br.

7) Do not use compact attribute on menu, ul, dl and ol.
8) Do not use frame attribute on iframe.
9) Do not use height attribute on th and td.
10) Do not use vspace and hspace attributes on img and object.
11) Do not use marginwidth and marginheight on iframe.
12) Do not use noshade on hr.
13) Do not use rules attribute on table.
14) Do not use scrolling attribute on iframe.
15) Do not use size attribute on hr.
16) Do not use type attribute on li and ul.
17) Do not use valign attribute on col, tbody, tfoot, thead ,tr , td, and th.
18) Do not use width attribute on table, col, hr, colgroup, pre, td, and th.

Conclusion

I hope this book has helped you learn about HTML. In writing it, I applied Pareto's law, also known as the 80/20 Rule. Understanding this law is helpful when learning any new language, especially a software language like HTML. You can learn 80% of the most used and most effective features of HTML in 4 hours, and I believe you have. To learn the next 20%, visit us online at http://www.whatshtml.com.

About the Author

John Rouda is an IT professional and Computer Science Professor. He has worked with HTML since the late 90's and spent seven years running a small web design/hosting firm until selling it. Currently, he manages a team of web developers and teaches as an adjunct faculty member at York Technical College and at Winthrop University. John currently has over 50 mobile apps in the Apple Appstore as well as over 20 in the Google Play Marketplace. He holds two master degrees, one in Business Administration and one in Computer Science.

John is married to a wonderful wife and has a beautiful family that he dearly loves. You can find out more about John at http://www.johnrouda.com or follow him on twitter @johnrouda.

Appendix A – HTML Tags

Tag	Description
<!--...-->	Defines a comment
<!DOCTYPE>	Defines the document type
<a>	Defines a hyperlink
<abbr>	Defines an abbreviation
<address>	Defines contact information for the author/owner of a document
<area>	Defines an area inside an image-map
<article>	Defines an article
<aside>	Defines content aside from the page content
<audio>	Defines sound content
<b>	Defines bold text
<base>	Specifies the base URL/target for all relative URLs in a document
<bdi>	Isolates a part of text that might be formatted in a different direction from other text outside it
<bdo>	Overrides the current text direction
<big>	Not supported in HTML5. Defines

	big text
<blockquote>	Defines a section that is quoted from another source
<body>	Defines the document's body
 	Defines a single line break
<button>	Defines a clickable button
<canvas>	Used to draw graphics, on the fly, via scripting (usually JavaScript)
<caption>	Defines a table caption
<center>	Not supported in HTML5. Deprecated in HTML 4.01. Defines centered text
<cite>	Defines the title of a work
<code>	Defines a piece of computer code
<col>	Specifies column properties for each column within a <colgroup> element
<colgroup>	Specifies a group of one or more columns in a table for formatting
<command>	Defines a command button that a user can invoke
<datalist>	Specifies a list of pre-defined options for input controls
<dd>	Defines a description of an item in a

	definition list
<del>	Defines text that has been deleted from a document
<details>	Defines additional details that the user can view or hide
<dfn>	Defines a definition term
<div>	Defines a section in a document
<dl>	Defines a definition list
<dt>	Defines a term (an item) in a definition list
<em>	Defines emphasized text
<embed>	Defines a container for an external (non-HTML) application
<fieldset>	Groups related elements in a form
<figcaption>	Defines a caption for a <figure> element
<figure>	Specifies self-contained content
<font>	Not supported in HTML5. Deprecated in HTML 4.01. Defines font, color, and size for text
<footer>	Defines a footer for a document or section
<form>	Defines an HTML form for user input

<frame>	Not supported in HTML5. Defines a window (a frame) in a frameset
<frameset>	Not supported in HTML5. Defines a set of frames
<h1> to <h6>	Defines HTML headings
<head>	Defines information about the document
<header>	Defines a header for a document or section
<hgroup>	Groups heading (<h1> to <h6>) elements
<hr>	Defines a thematic change in the content
<html>	Defines the root of an HTML document
<i>	Defines a part of text in an alternate voice or mood
<iframe>	Defines an inline frame
<img>	Defines an image
<input>	Defines an input control
<ins>	Defines a text that has been inserted into a document
<kbd>	Defines keyboard input

<keygen>	Defines a key-pair generator field (for forms)
<label>	Defines a label for an <input> element
<legend>	Defines a caption for a <fieldset>, < figure>, or <details> element
<li>	Defines a list item
<link>	Defines the relationship between a document and an external resource (most used to link to style sheets)
<map>	Defines a client-side image-map
<mark>	Defines marked/highlighted text
<menu>	Defines a list/menu of commands
<meta>	Defines metadata about an HTML document
<meter>	Defines a scalar measurement within a known range (a gauge)
<nav>	Defines navigation links
<noframes>	Not supported in HTML5. Defines an alternate content for users that do not support frames
<noscript>	Defines an alternate content for users that do not support client-side scripts

<object>	Defines an embedded object
<ol>	Defines an ordered list
<optgroup>	Defines a group of related options in a drop-down list
<option>	Defines an option in a drop-down list
<output>	Defines the result of a calculation
<p>	Defines a paragraph
<param>	Defines a parameter for an object
<pre>	Defines preformatted text
<progress>	Represents the progress of a task
<q>	Defines a short quotation
<rp>	Defines what to show in browsers that do not support ruby annotations
<rt>	Defines an explanation/pronunciation of characters (for East Asian typography)
<ruby>	Defines a ruby annotation (for East Asian typography)
<s>	Defines text that is no longer correct
<samp>	Defines sample output from a

	computer program
<script>	Defines a client-side script
<section>	Defines a section in a document
<select>	Defines a drop-down list
<small>	Defines smaller text
<source>	Defines multiple media resources for media elements (<video> and <audio>)
<span>	Defines a section in a document
<strike>	Not supported in HTML5. Deprecated in HTML 4.01. Defines strikethrough text
<strong>	Defines important text
<style>	Defines style information for a document
<sub>	Defines subscripted text
<summary>	Defines a visible heading for a <details> element
<sup>	Defines superscripted text
<table>	Defines a table
<tbody>	Groups the body content in a table
<td>	Defines a cell in a table
<textarea>	Defines a multiline input control

	(text area)
<tfoot>	Groups the footer content in a table
<th>	Defines a header cell in a table
<thead>	Groups the header content in a table
<time>	Defines a date/time
<title>	Defines a title for the document
<tr>	Defines a row in a table
<track>	Defines text tracks for media elements (<video> and <audio>)
<u>	Defines text that should be stylistically different from normal text
<ul>	Defines an unordered list
<var>	Defines a variable
<video>	Defines a video or movie
<wbr>	Defines a possible line-break

Appendix B - CSS

Property	Description
@keyframes	Defines the animation
animation	A shorthand property for all the animation properties below, except the animation-play-state property
animation-name	Defines a name for the @keyframes animation
animation-duration	Defines how many seconds or milliseconds an animation takes to complete one cycle
animation-timing-function	Defines the speed curve of the animation
animation-delay	Defines when the animation will start
animation-iteration-count	Defines the number of times an animation should be played
animation-direction	Defines whether or not the animation should play in reverse on alternate cycles

animation-play-state	Defines whether the animation is running or paused
background	Sets all the background properties in one declaration
background-attachment	Sets whether a background image is fixed or scrolls with the rest of the page
background-color	Sets the background color of an element
background-image	Sets the background image for an element
background-position	Sets the starting position of a background image
background-repeat	Sets how a background image will be repeated
background-clip	Defines the painting area of the background
background-origin	Defines the positioning area of the background images
background-size	Defines the size of the background images
border	Sets all the border properties in one declaration
border-bottom	Sets all the bottom border properties in one declaration
border-	Sets the color of the bottom

bottom-color	border
border-bottom-style	Sets the style of the bottom border
border-bottom-width	Sets the width of the bottom border
border-color	Sets the color of the four borders
border-left	Sets all the left border properties in one declaration
border-left-color	Sets the color of the left border
border-left-style	Sets the style of the left border
border-left-width	Sets the width of the left border
border-right	Sets all the right border properties in one declaration
border-right-color	Sets the color of the right border
border-right-style	Sets the style of the right border
border-right-width	Sets the width of the right border
border-style	Sets the style of the four borders
border-top	Sets all the top border properties

	in one declaration
border-top-color	Sets the color of the top border
border-top-style	Sets the style of the top border
border-top-width	Sets the width of the top border
border-width	Sets the width of the four borders
outline	Sets all the outline properties in one declaration
outline-color	Sets the color of an outline
outline-style	Sets the style of an outline
outline-width	Sets the width of an outline
border-bottom-left-radius	Defines the shape of the border of the bottom-left corner
border-bottom-right-radius	Defines the shape of the border of the bottom-right corner
border-image	A shorthand property for setting all the border-image-* properties
border-image-outset	Defines the amount by which the border image area extends beyond the border box
border-image-	Defines whether the image-

repeat	border should be repeated, rounded or stretched
border-image-slice	Defines the inward offsets of the image-border
border-image-source	Defines an image to be used as a border
border-image-width	Defines the widths of the image-border
border-radius	A shorthand property for setting all the four border-*-radius properties
border-top-left-radius	Defines the shape of the border of the top-left corner
border-top-right-radius	Defines the shape of the border of the top-right corner
box-decoration-break	
box-shadow	Attaches one or more drop-shadows to the box
overflow-x	Defines whether or not to clip the left/right edges of the content, if it overflows the element's content area
overflow-y	Defines whether or not to clip the top/bottom edges of the content,

	if it overflows the element's content area
overflow-style	Defines the preferred scrolling method for elements that overflow
rotation	Rotates an element around a given point defined by the rotation-point property
rotation-point	Defines a point as an offset from the top left border edge
color-profile	Permits the specification of a source color profile other than the default
opacity	Sets the opacity level for an element
rendering-intent	Permits the specification of a color profile rendering intent other than the default
bookmark-label	Defines the label of the bookmark
bookmark-level	Defines the level of the bookmark
bookmark-target	Defines the target of the bookmark link
float-offset	Pushes floated elements in the opposite direction of the where

	they have been floated with float
hyphenate-after	Defines the minimum number of characters in a hyphenated word after the hyphenation character
hyphenate-before	Defines the minimum number of characters in a hyphenated word before the hyphenation character
hyphenate-character	Defines a string that is shown when a hyphenate-break occurs
hyphenate-lines	Indicates the maximum number of successive hyphenated lines in an element
hyphenate-resource	Defines a comma-separated list of external resources that can help the browser determine hyphenation points
hyphens	Sets how to split words to improve the layout of paragraphs
image-resolution	Defines the correct resolution of images
marks	Adds crop and/or cross marks to the document
string-set	
height	Sets the height of an element
max-height	Sets the maximum height of an

	element
max-width	Sets the maximum width of an element
min-height	Sets the minimum height of an element
min-width	Sets the minimum width of an element
width	Sets the width of an element
box-align	Defines how to align the child elements of a box
box-direction	Defines in which direction the children of a box are displayed
box-flex	Defines whether the children of a box is flexible or inflexible in size
box-flex-group	Assigns flexible elements to flex groups
box-lines	Defines whether columns will go onto a new line whenever it runs out of space in the parent box
box-ordinal-group	Defines the display order of the child elements of a box
box-orient	Defines whether the children of a box should be laid out horizontally or vertically
box-pack	Defines the horizontal position in horizontal boxes and the vertical

	position in vertical boxes
font	Sets all the font properties in one declaration
font-family	Defines the font family for text
font-size	Defines the font size of text
font-style	Defines the font style for text
font-variant	Defines whether or not a text should be displayed in a small-caps font
font-weight	Defines the weight of a font
@font-face	A rule that allows websites to download and use fonts other than the "web-safe" fonts
font-size-adjust	Preserves the readability of text when font fallback occurs
font-stretch	Selects a normal, condensed, or expanded face from a font family
content	Used with the :before and :after pseudo-elements, to insert generated content
counter-increment	Increments one or more counters
counter-reset	Creates or resets one or more counters

quotes	Sets the type of quotation marks for embedded quotations
crop	Allows a replaced element to be just a rectangular area of an object, instead of the whole object
move-to	Causes an element to be removed from the flow and reinserted at a later point in the document
page-policy	Determines which page-based occurance of a given element is applied to a counter or string value
grid-columns	Defines the width of each column in a grid
grid-rows	Defines the height of each column in a grid
target	A shorthand property for setting the target-name, target-new, and target-position properties
target-name	Defines where to open links (target destination)
target-new	Defines whether new destination links should open in a new window or in a new tab of an existing window
target-	Defines where new destination

position	links should be placed
alignment-adjust	Allows more precise alignment of elements
alignment-baseline	Defines how an inline-level element is aligned with respect to its parent
baseline-shift	Allows repositioning of the dominant-baseline relative to the dominant-baseline
dominant-baseline	Defines a scaled-baseline-table
drop-initial-after-adjust	Sets the alignment point of the drop initial for the primary connection point
drop-initial-after-align	Sets which alignment line within the initial line box is used at the primary connection point with the initial letter box
drop-initial-before-adjust	Sets the alignment point of the drop initial for the secondary connection point
drop-initial-before-align	Sets which alignment line within the initial line box is used at the secondary connection point with the initial letter box
drop-initial-	Controls the partial sinking of the

size	initial letter
drop-initial-value	Activates a drop-initial effect
inline-box-align	Sets which line of a multi-line inline block align with the previous and next inline elements within a line
line-stacking	A shorthand property for setting the line-stacking-strategy, line-stacking-ruby, and line-stacking-shift properties
line-stacking-ruby	Sets the line stacking method for block elements containing ruby annotation elements
line-stacking-shift	Sets the line stacking method for block elements containing elements with base-shift
line-stacking-strategy	Sets the line stacking strategy for stacked line boxes within a containing block element
text-height	Sets the block-progression dimension of the text content area of an inline box
list-style	Sets all the properties for a list in one declaration
list-style-image	Defines an image as the list-item marker

list-style-position	Defines if the list-item markers should appear inside or outside the content flow
list-style-type	Defines the type of list-item marker
margin	Sets all the margin properties in one declaration
margin-bottom	Sets the bottom margin of an element
margin-left	Sets the left margin of an element
margin-right	Sets the right margin of an element
margin-top	Sets the top margin of an element
marquee-direction	Sets the direction of the moving content
marquee-play-count	Sets how many times the content move
marquee-speed	Sets how fast the content scrolls
marquee-style	Sets the style of the moving content
column-count	Defines the number of columns an element should be divided into

column-fill	Defines how to fill columns
column-gap	Defines the gap between the columns
column-rule	A shorthand property for setting all the column-rule-* properties
column-rule-color	Defines the color of the rule between columns
column-rule-style	Defines the style of the rule between columns
column-rule-width	Defines the width of the rule between columns
column-span	Defines how many columns an element should span across
column-width	Defines the width of the columns
columns	A shorthand property for setting column-width and column-count
padding	Sets all the padding properties in one declaration
padding-bottom	Sets the bottom padding of an element
padding-left	Sets the left padding of an element
padding-right	Sets the right padding of an element
padding-top	Sets the top padding of an

	element
fit	Gives a hint for how to scale a replaced element if neither its width nor its height property is auto
fit-position	Determines the alignment of the object inside the box
image-orientation	Defines a rotation in the right or clockwise direction that a user agent applies to an image
page	Defines a particular type of page where an element SHOULD be displayed
size	Defines the size and orientation of the containing box for page content
bottom	Defines the bottom position of a positioned element
clear	Defines which sides of an element where other floating elements are not allowed
clip	Clips an absolutely positioned element
cursor	Defines the type of cursor to be displayed
display	Defines how a certain HTML

	element should be displayed
float	Defines whether or not a box should float
left	Defines the left position of a positioned element
overflow	Defines what happens if content overflows an element's box
position	Defines the type of positioning method used for an element (static, relative, absolute or fixed)
right	Defines the right position of a positioned element
top	Defines the top position of a positioned element
visibility	Defines whether or not an element is visible
z-index	Sets the stack order of a positioned element
orphans	Sets the minimum number of lines that must be left at the bottom of a page when a page break occurs inside an element
page-break-after	Sets the page-breaking behavior after an element
page-break-before	Sets the page-breaking behavior before an element

page-break-inside	Sets the page-breaking behavior inside an element
widows	Sets the minimum number of lines that must be left at the top of a page when a page break occurs inside an element
ruby-align	Controls the text alignment of the ruby text and ruby base contents relative to each other
ruby-overhang	Determines whether, and on which side, ruby text is allowed to partially overhang any adjacent text in addition to its own base, when the ruby text is wider than the ruby base
ruby-position	Controls the position of the ruby text with respect to its base
ruby-span	Controls the spanning behavior of annotation elements
mark	A shorthand property for setting the mark-before and mark-after properties
mark-after	Allows named markers to be attached to the audio stream
mark-before	Allows named markers to be attached to the audio stream

phonemes	Defines a phonetic pronunciation for the text contained by the corresponding element
rest	A shorthand property for setting the rest-before and rest-after properties
rest-after	Defines a rest or prosodic boundary to be observed after speaking an element's content
rest-before	Defines a rest or prosodic boundary to be observed before speaking an element's content
voice-balance	Defines the balance between left and right channels
voice-duration	Defines how long it should take to render the selected element's content
voice-pitch	Defines the average pitch (a frequency) of the speaking voice
voice-pitch-range	Defines variation in average pitch
voice-rate	Controls the speaking rate
voice-stress	Indicates the strength of emphasis to be applied
voice-volume	Refers to the amplitude of the waveform output by the speech

	synthesises
border-collapse	Defines whether or not table borders should be collapsed
border-spacing	Defines the distance between the borders of adjacent cells
caption-side	Defines the placement of a table caption
empty-cells	Defines whether or not to display borders and background on empty cells in a table
table-layout	Sets the layout algorithm to be used for a table
color	Sets the color of text
direction	Defines the text direction/writing direction
letter-spacing	Increases or decreases the space between characters in a text
line-height	Sets the line height
text-align	Defines the horizontal alignment of text
text-decoration	Defines the decoration added to text
text-indent	Defines the indentation of the first line in a text-block

text-transform	Controls the capitalization of text
vertical-align	Sets the vertical alignment of an element
white-space	Defines how white-space inside an element is handled
word-spacing	Increases or decreases the space between words in a text
hanging-punctuation	Defines whether a punctuation character may be placed outside the line box
punctuation-trim	Defines whether a punctuation character should be trimmed
text-align-last	Describes how the last line of a block or a line right before a forced line break is aligned when text-align is "justify"
text-justify	Defines the justification method used when text-align is "justify"
text-outline	Defines a text outline
text-overflow	Defines what should happen when text overflows the containing element
text-shadow	Adds shadow to text
text-wrap	Defines line breaking rules for text

word-break	Defines line breaking rules for non-CJK scripts
word-wrap	Allows long, unbreakable words to be broken and wrap to the next line
transform	Applies a 2D or 3D transformation to an element
transform-origin	Allows you to change the position on transformed elements
transform-style	Defines how nested elements are rendered in 3D space
perspective	Defines the perspective on how 3D elements are viewed
perspective-origin	Defines the bottom position of 3D elements
backface-visibility	Defines whether or not an element should be visible when not facing the screen
transition	A shorthand property for setting the four transition properties
transition-property	Defines the name of the CSS property the transition effect is for
transition-duration	Defines how many seconds or milliseconds a transition effect takes to complete

transition-timing-function	Defines the speed curve of the transition effect
transition-delay	Defines when the transition effect will start
appearance	Allows you to make an element look like a standard user interface element
box-sizing	Allows you to define certain elements to fit an area in a certain way
icon	Provides the author the ability to style an element with an iconic equivalent
nav-down	Defines where to navigate when using the arrow-down navigation key
nav-index	Defines the tabbing order for an element
nav-left	Defines where to navigate when using the arrow-left navigation key
nav-right	Defines where to navigate when using the arrow-right navigation key
nav-up	Defines where to navigate when using the arrow-up navigation key

outline-offset   Offsets an outline and draws beyond the borders edge

resize   Determines whether or not an element is resizable by the user

Appendix C – HTML Entities

Reserved Characters in HTML

Result	Entity Number	Entity Name
"	"	"
'	'	'
&	&	&
<	<	<
>	>	>

Note: Entity names are case sensitive!

ISO 8859-1 Symbols

Result	Entity Number	Entity Name
¡	¡	¡
¢	¢	¢
£	£	£
¤	¤	¤
¥	¥	¥
¦	¦	¦
§	§	§
¨	¨	¨
©	©	©
ª	ª	ª
«	«	«
¬	¬	¬
	­	­
®	®	®
¯	¯	¯
°	°	°
±	±	±

2	&#178;	&sup2;
3	&#179;	&sup3;
´	&#180;	&acute;
µ	&#181;	&micro;
¶	&#182;	&para;
·	&#183;	&middot;
¸	&#184;	&cedil;
1	&#185;	&sup1;
o	&#186;	&ordm;
»	&#187;	&raquo;
¼	&#188;	&frac14;
½	&#189;	&frac12;
¾	&#190;	&frac34;
¿	&#191;	&iquest;
×	&#215;	&times;
÷	&#247;	&divide;

ISO 8859-1 Characters

Character	Entity Number	Entity Name
À	&#192;	&Agrave;
Á	&#193;	&Aacute;
Â	&#194;	&Acirc;
Ã	&#195;	&Atilde;
Ä	&#196;	&Auml;
Å	&#197;	&Aring;
Æ	&#198;	&AElig;
Ç	&#199;	&Ccedil;
È	&#200;	&Egrave;
É	&#201;	&Eacute;
Ê	&#202;	&Ecirc;
Ë	&#203;	&Euml;
Ì	&#204;	&Igrave;

Í	Í	Í
Î	Î	Î
Ï	Ï	Ï
Ð	Ð	Ð
Ñ	Ñ	Ñ
Ò	Ò	Ò
Ó	Ó	Ó
Ô	Ô	Ô
Õ	Õ	Õ
Ö	Ö	Ö
Ø	Ø	Ø
Ù	Ù	Ù
Ú	Ú	Ú
Û	Û	Û
Ü	Ü	Ü
Ý	Ý	Ý
Þ	Þ	Þ
ß	ß	ß
à	à	à
á	á	á
â	â	â
ã	ã	ã
ä	ä	ä
å	å	å
æ	æ	æ
ç	ç	ç
è	è	è
é	é	é
ê	ê	ê
ë	ë	ë
ì	ì	ì
í	í	í
î	î	î
ï	ï	ï

ð	&#240;	&eth;
ñ	&#241;	&ntilde;
ò	&#242;	&ograve;
ó	&#243;	&oacute;
ô	&#244;	&ocirc;
õ	&#245;	&otilde;
ö	&#246;	&ouml;
ø	&#248;	&oslash;
ù	&#249;	&ugrave;
ú	&#250;	&uacute;
û	&#251;	&ucirc;
ü	&#252;	&uuml;
ý	&#253;	&yacute;
þ	&#254;	&thorn;
ÿ	&#255;	&yuml;